Primary Sources of World Cultures™

JAPAN

A PRIMARY SOURCE CULTURAL GUIDE

Meg Greene

The Rosen Publishing Group's
PowerPlus Books™
New York

For Genevive and Sienna

Published in 2005 by The Rosen Publishing Group, Inc.
29 East 21st Street, New York, NY 10010

First Edition

Library of Congress Cataloging-in-Publication Data

Greene, Meg.
Japan: a primary source cultural guide/Meg Greene.—1st ed.
    p. cm.—(Primary sources of world cultures)
ISBN 1-4042-2912-4 (library binding)
1. Japan—Juvenile literature. I. Title. II. Series
DS806.G74 2005
952—dc22

2004000017

Manufactured in the United States of America

On the cover: Background: Seventeenth-century poem by Matsuo Basho, one of the greatest Japanese haiku poets. Left: Osaka Castle, Osaka, Japan. Right: A young girl in a kimono from Matsushima, Japan.

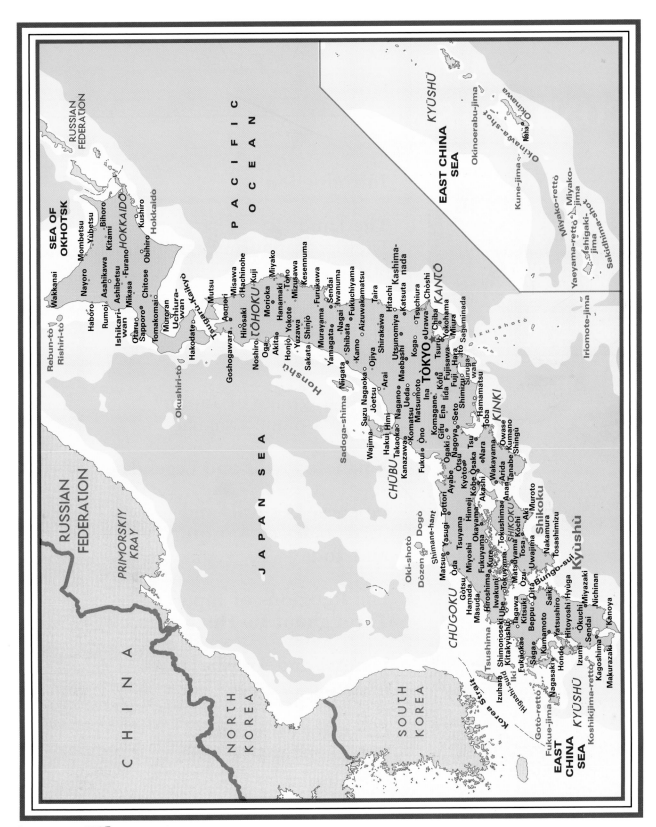

APR 1 4 2005

CONTENTS

INTRODUCTION

J apan is one of the most unique and intriguing countries in the world. This small nation, consisting of a number of islands, is often thought by its residents to be a divine land, blessed by the early gods. It is easy to see why the Japanese feel this way about their country. From its stunningly lush forests and the majestic snow-capped tip of Mount Fuji to the fertile rice fields and the beautiful ocean waters that surround it, Japan is a spectacular land of great majesty and natural beauty.

The Japanese people enjoy a rich and fascinating history dating back thousands of years. One of the most distinctive features of Japanese culture is the capacity of the Japanese to borrow and adapt from other cultures. Out of these borrowings has been created something entirely new and distinctive, something that is truly Japanese. The end result is a rich mix of an old and vibrant history and cultural traditions with very modern elements.

For centuries, Japan chose to remain an isolated nation, looking only to China for the creation of its government, its education, and its religious beliefs. But with the arrival of American commodore

At left, a bullet train speeds down the track past Mount Fuji. Known in Japan as Shinkansen, the bullet trains run at speeds up to 185 miles per hour (300 kilometers per hour). At right, the neon lights of Shinjuku light up western Tokyo. The ward (a type of district) of Shinjuku is home to Tokyo's city hall.

Tokyo is famous for its constant traffic and gridlocked rush hours. On a sunny afternoon in Tokyo, shoppers enjoy the peace of car-empty streets on a *hokosha tengoku* (pedestrian's paradise) holiday.

Matthew Perry in 1853 and the establishment of diplomatic ties with the United States, Japan became one of the very first Asian nations to modernize. By borrowing Western ways, the Japanese changed their government, their school systems, their economy, and even the way they dressed and wore their hair. This not only enabled Japan to compete with the West, but it also allowed it to establish itself as a world power. Yet, in spite of the country's modernization, Japan remains at heart a very conservative nation, one whose people still look to tradition and history to help them make their way in the modern world.

In Japan, day-to-day living mixes old and new and blends East and West with a flair that is distinctly Japanese. For instance, fast-food restaurants are a lively mix of Western and Japanese influences. Yoshinoya's gyudon beef bowl competes in popularity with a McDonald's hamburger. A typical street scene in Tokyo might consist of a small Shinto shrine where people spend a moment or two offering prayers for a loved one. Many people offer bouquets of flowers, often stuck in small Coca-Cola

In this illustration from the series called Illustrations to 100 Poems by 100 Poets, by Gontchunagon Masafusa, three men are admiring cherry blossoms. Meanwhile, two women are fetching water and other visitors are climbing up the path.

bottles, one of the most recognizable symbols of Western popular culture. And while the majority of Japanese wear Western dress every day, the traditional kimono is still worn to commemorate special holidays and celebrations in Japan.

While Japan has integrated much from Western culture into its own, the West has also been influenced by the Japanese, especially in the areas of technology and popular culture. Japanese electronics such as televisions, film and digital cameras, VCRs, DVD players, and other appliances are considered to be among the best in the world. The Japanese are often leaders in world technology. They develop products months and even years ahead of many Western companies. For example, the growing popularity of cell phones is due, in large part, to Japanese technology. In fact, by the time a trend—such as cell phones that take pictures— arrives in the West, the Japanese have already moved on to something else, such as cell phones that double as video cameras.

A young man sings a song in a karaoke club in Tokyo. Karaoke began in Japan in the late 1970s. It has become increasingly popular in Western countries since the 1990s.

Popular culture in North America has been heavily influenced by the Japanese. Video game equipment such as the XBox and Nintendo Game Boy and popular video games such as the *Legend of Zelda* are Japanese in origin. In some cases, popular Japanese video game characters, such as Pokémon, have also been featured in films, comic books, and trading cards. Some Japanese cartoon programs, such as *Sailor Moon*, have found new audiences on this side of the international dateline. And both adults and children enjoy karaoke, in which a person sings songs accompanied by a karaoke machine that plays pre-recorded music.

Even though Japan is a world power, the Japanese are very dependent on other countries for many of their goods. For instance, Japan imports more than 31 percent of its machinery and

The *Legend of Zelda* video games feature a young hero named Link who goes on many missions to save Princess Zelda. The *Zelda* games have influenced many other video games.

This is the closed storefront of a restaurant in the Ryogiku section of Tokyo, which was once an arena for sumo wrestlers. In Japan, sumo wrestling is a very popular contemporary martial art.

heavy equipment, 12 percent of its food, and a little more than 19 percent of its mineral fuels, such as coal and natural gas.

But many nations rely on Japanese exports, too. Japan is second only to the United States in terms of its industrial exports and is also the world's leading exporter of cars, which include such companies as Toyota and Nissan. In addition, Japan exports electrical machinery, office equipment, semi-conductors, and appliances worldwide.

Japan is also a land of startling contrasts. While great attention is spent by the Japanese government to protect its immense wealth of natural and cultural treasures, the Japanese continue to borrow from other nations and cultures. Japan is a country with high standards of living, yet its approximately 127 million residents are crammed into an area smaller than the European country of Portugal or the American state of Montana. It is these unique contrasts and differences, along with its wealth of art, architecture, and history, that make Japan a continuing source of interest for scholars, visitors, and the Japanese people themselves.

THE LAND

The Geography and Environment of Japan

L
ying midway between the equator and the North Pole, Japan is made up of a crescent-shaped series of islands located along the eastern coast of the Asian continent. These islands are actually the exposed tops of massive undersea ridges that jut out from the floor of the Pacific Ocean. The Pacific Ocean lies to the east. To the west is the Sea of Japan.

Japan occupies only 145,709 square miles (377,835 square kilometers). There are four main Japanese islands: Hokkaido, Honshu, Shikoku, and Kyushu, which stretch approximately 1,500 miles (2,400 km) from the northeast to the southwest. Honshu is the largest of the four, making up approximately three-fifths, or 60 percent, of the total area of Japan. The majority of major Japanese cities, such as Tokyo, Osaka, Kobe, Kyoto, and Yokohama, and about four-fifths, or 80 percent, of the country's more than 127 million inhabitants live on Honshu. Together, the four main islands amount to about 95 percent of Japan's territory.

Making up the remaining 5 percent are more than 4,000 smaller islands. These include Ogasawara-gunto, Daito-jima, Minami-jima, Okinotorishima, the Ryukyu Islands, and Nansei-shoto. Altogether, Japan is about 1,860 miles (3,000 km) long and approximately 200 miles (320 km)

At left is an aerial view of a rice paddy in Shiga, Japan. Rice is the world's third-largest crop. Above is a view of Tokyo and the Rainbow Bridge, which extends across Tokyo Bay. The cities of Yokohama, Chiba, Kawasaki, and Yokosuka are also located on Tokyo Bay.

wide. No matter where a person stands in Japan, he or she is never more than 93 miles (150 km) from the sea.

As an island nation, Japan has no land borders with any other country. To the west, the Sea of Japan separates Japan from North and South Korea; across the Sea of Japan to the north is Russia; across the East China Sea to the west is China; and southwest of Japan's Ryukyu Islands are Taiwan and the Philippines. The vast waters of the Pacific Ocean wash up on the eastern and southeastern shores of Japan. More than 4,000 miles (6,400 km) to the east is North America.

Japan is located in one of the most geologically unstable regions in the world. The country experiences some 1,500 tremors annually, though most of them are minor. However, major earthquakes, such as those that struck Tokyo and Yokohama in 1923 and Kobe in 1995, have caused considerable loss of life and widespread destruction.

Japan also has approximately six volcanic regions that range from the far north to the far south. Violent volcanic eruptions occur with frequency. There are a total of 186 volcanoes in Japan. Of these, approximately 108 are active, including Mount Mihara on Izu Oshima Island, Mount Asama on the border between Nagano and Gunma Prefectures, and Mount Aso in Kumamoto Prefecture. Japan has almost 7 percent of the world's approximately 1,562 active volcanoes, even though the country occupies only about one-four hundredth of the world's land area.

Another distinctive landform found in the volcanic areas are calderas. These are large, circular, basin-shaped depressions located especially in northeastern

The destruction of the 1923 earthquake in Tokyo was devastating. This photo of the Ginza shows Tokyo's main shopping area in ruins.

Steam rises from snowcapped volcanoes in Daisetsuzan National Park in Hokkaido. Daisetsuzan is Japan's largest national park.

and southwestern Japan. Many calderas are filled with water, such as Lakes Kutcharo, Towada, and Ashinoko. Japan is also known for its wonderful hot springs, which result from volcanic activity heating water beneath the surface of the earth. These areas are popular getaway spots both for the Japanese and for foreign visitors. Thermal resorts and spas, or *onsens,* are noted for their communal bathhouse facilities. These are considered to be therapeutic and extremely relaxing.

A Diverse Landscape

Earthquakes and volcanoes have created a rugged landscape with hills and mountains covering more than 80 percent of the land surface of Japan. The largest and highest group of mountains, known as the Japanese Alps, is in central Honshu. From this range, mountain chains extend northward to Hokkaido and southwest to Shikoku and Kyushu. Mount Fuji, at 12,388 feet (3,776 meters), is the highest

Colorful autumn leaves in a forest near Lake Chuzenji-Ko. Many city-dwellers spend their weekends camping or hiking in the forests during the fall season.

peak in Japan. A giant volcano, Mount Fuji is also a national landmark. It is considered by many to be the symbol of Japan. The volcano is also a popular tourist site. Each year, thousands journey to see the once-active volcano, and many hike to its top to look at the breathtaking view.

A number of river valleys and lowland plains also distinguish the geography of Japan. These plains have been formed by river deposits and lie along the coastlines. Japan's rivers are also very short; only two are more than 200 miles (322 km) long: the Shinano and the Tone, both of which are on Honshu. Although most of these small rivers are not navigable and are thus useless for commerce and transportation, they provide water for irrigation and drinking. The Japanese have also harnessed some of these rivers to generate hydroelectric power. These rivers commonly overflow, especially during the typhoon season. There are not many lakes in Japan. The largest is Biwa, located in the west-central region of Honshu.

Only 25 percent of the land surface of Japan is relatively flat. It is along these coastal lowlands where the majority of the population lives. Because so much of the land is unsuitable for farming, Japan is an urban nation. In fact, it is among the most urbanized countries in the world. In 1920, more than four-fifths, or 80 percent, of the

Japanese people still lived in the countryside. By 1998, however, approximately 77 percent of the inhabitants lived in cities, most of which had populations of more than 30,000. About 80 percent of Japan's total population lives on Honshu, 12 percent on Kyushu, 5 percent on Hokkaido, and 3 percent on Shikoku.

The greatest concentration of the population, or roughly 42 percent, lives in the Tokaido megalopolis, which includes six of the seven largest cities in Japan. This area extends for 350 miles (563 km), from Tokyo and Yokohama in the Kanto Plain, westward along the Pacific Coast through Nagoya and Kyoto, and on to Osaka and Kobe. The Kanto Plain, which lies east of the Japanese Alps, is Japan's largest lowland region. It is an important agricultural and industrial center. The Osaka Plain, which lies to the south and west of the Kanto Plain, is the leading manufacturing and commercial region in Japan. It also houses many of the leading producers of software, electrical components, and chemicals.

The Climate

Japan experiences a variety of climates, due in part to its closeness to water and mountainous terrain. In the mountains, winters can be cold, with biting winds sweeping down from the vast Siberian plain. Heavy snows—among some of the deepest in the world—are deposited on the west coast, while the east coast enjoys sunnier and warmer weather. During the summer, Japan receives southwest winds moving in from the Pacific Ocean. This makes Japanese summers along the east

Visitors at the New Otani Gardens get caught in a typhoon (tropical cyclone). Typhoons involve high speed, swirling winds and thunderstorms.

On a hazy day in May, the spectacularly beautiful island of Miyajima—just a thirty-minute boat ride from Hiroshima—offers dramatic views of Inland Sea.

coast hot and humid, while the west coast remains somewhat cooler.

The cycle of the seasons brings frequent, often sharp changes in the weather. This especially affects the west coast during the spring and autumn. The climate there is affected by two ocean currents: the warm Kuroshio, or Japan Current, from the south, and the cold Oyashio, or Okhotsk Current, from the north. The Oyashio also reduces hot summer temperatures and often creates deep and dense fog banks along the northeastern coasts of Honshu and Hokkaido.

Virtually all of Japan averages more than 40 inches (100 centimeters) of precipitation per year. The rainy season occurs in June and September, though some precipitation occurs throughout the year. The main rainy season in June is called the *baiu* or *tsuyu*, and can bring days of continuous rain. Known as "plum rains," these downpours aid the cultivation of rice. The September rainy season, called the *shurin*, is associated with occasional typhoons, which are similar to the tropical storms and hurricanes that hit the Caribbean, southeastern North America, and the Gulf coast. When typhoons strike, they bring destructive floods and landslides. They also restore water levels, which drop during the relatively dry months of late summer. Typhoons account for roughly one-third, or 33 percent, of the annual rainfall on the Pacific coast of Asia. They are closely monitored by Japanese weather agencies.

Plant and Animal Life

There is a great variety of trees, shrubs, and flowering plants in Japan. Forests cover almost 75 percent of the country. There are three forest zones in Japan. The island of Hokkaido is home to trees such as pine, cedar, fir, alder, aspen, and spruce. Maple,

A young girl stands under a blossoming cherry tree. In Japan, cherry blossoms are called sakura. Sakura represent the short-lived beauty of life. Sakura are often depicted in Japanese art and poetry.

beech, willow, holly, and mulberry trees grow in the northern and central Honshu region. Bamboo, tea plants, wax trees, and palm trees flourish in the southern regions of Japan. Human activity has destroyed or reduced many plant species, but the Japanese have introduced new species from the Asian mainland. They have also preserved virgin, or untouched, forests in limited areas.

One of the most popular trees in Japan is the cherry tree, which is the national symbol of Japan. Sakura, or cherry blossoms, are native to Japan and are a symbol of spring, life, and beauty in Japan. They bloom for a very short time in the early spring when everything is alive and new, and they are greatly cherished by the Japanese. Traditional stories explain the origin of these delicate, beautiful trees. According to one legend, cherry trees came to Japan when a Japanese goddess named Konohanasakuyahime planted cherry tree seeds high on top of Mount Fuji.

Although animal life in Japan is not nearly as diverse as the vegetation, there is still a great variety. Bears, badgers, wild boars, otters, deer, foxes, monkeys, and

Koi is a type of common carp with colorful scales. In Japan, koi are kept in garden ponds and pools for decorative purposes. Koi are either white, yellow, red, black, or blue. Their scales often have a glittering metallic sheen. Since the seventeenth century, breeding techniques have been used to control the koi's appearance.

seals are abundant. Among the many different bird species are hawks, pheasants, doves, owls, and woodpeckers. Songbirds such as swallows, house swallows, and thrushes are also plentiful. One songbird in particular, the bush warbler or *uguisu*, is very much admired. Reptile life includes a variety of snakes and lizards.

Aquatic life in Japan ranges from whales, porpoises, sea turtles, and tortoises to many different kinds of fish including salmon, sardines, sea bream, tuna, squid, mackerel, and cod. Such an abundance of fish makes the fishing industry an important part of the Japanese economy. There are farms that raise goldfish and colorful carp (koi), which are placed in Japanese gardens and decorative ponds. Commercial fisheries in which various fish, eels, and pearl oysters are raised and sold are also very important in Japan.

Many of the natural resources of Japan, like those of other countries around the world, are endangered. Pollution from Japanese power plant emissions has caused

Two Japanese cranes call out in unison at the Tsurui Crane Sanctuary in Hokkaido, the northern island of Japan. In ancient Japan, cranes were highly admired. They were even fed and protected by royalty.

acid rain. As a result, the acidification of lakes and reservoirs has ruined water quality and threatened aquatic life. As the Japanese are one of the largest consumers of fish and tropical timber, they have also contributed to the worldwide depletion of these resources. However, the Japanese government has enacted two laws to help preserve the environment: the Basic Environment Law, passed in 1993, and the Basic Environment Plan, passed in 1994.

As a result of these two efforts, the government shifted emphasis to activities that will encourage land conservation and the management of protected areas and wildlife. Already at the local and prefecture levels, programs have been instituted to raise awareness of the importance of the environment and the need to promote environmental education for Japanese citizens.

THE PEOPLE

2

Invention, Innovation, and Tradition

L ittle is known about the origins of the Japanese people. However, twentieth-century discoveries of early skeletal remains dating from about 8000 BC suggest that the Japanese descended from a Mongoloid people closely related to the Chinese and the Koreans. This has led historians to conclude that people first arrived in Japan from northeastern Asia, probably crossing over from the Korean peninsula, which is quite close to Japan. Yet, it is also possible that some early Japanese may have come from as far away as the South Pacific. They would have made their way to Japan by moving from island to island.

Origins

The first known settlers of Japan were the Jomon people, who flourished between 10,500 and 300 BC. The word "jomon," which means "cord-marked," refers to the distinctive ropelike markings that decorated the surfaces of their clay vessels. Jomon culture is also known as Tree culture because trees were an important element in building con-

struction, ceremonial ornaments, and for use as daily tools. The first Jomon people were hunter-gatherers; they never stayed in one place, but moved when they needed to find food.

At left, on an early summer day on an old street in Kyoto near Kiyomizu Temple, two *maiko* (apprentice geisha) walk down a busy street. Above, six kamikaze pilots pose for a picture in 1945. "Kamikaze" means "divine wind." Kamikaze pilots were sent on suicide missions during World War II. They used their own planes as bombs to attack U.S. and Allied ships.

This statue of a female deity is from the Jomon period. Jomon people created the earliest pottery in the world, dating back to the eleventh century BC.

The next wave of immigrants was the Yayoi people who arrived in about 350 BC from northern China. They are named for a district in modern-day Tokyo where archaeologists first unearthed remnants of their settlements. The Yayoi brought with them agriculture, a knowledge of metalworking with bronze and iron, and wheel-thrown, kiln-fired ceramics. They also brought a new religion that would eventually develop into Shinto. However, this would not happen for many, many years. The Yayoi lived in clans called *uji*. A clan is a group of people who either trace their history from a common ancestor or are united by a common interest.

During the period from AD 300 to 710, which is known as the Kofun, or Tumulus, period (named for the large tombs—kofun—which were built for political leaders), clans also played an important role. These groups formed important political treaties and established their center in the fertile Kinai Plain. The most powerful of these clans was the Yamato. Eventually, the Yamato gained power over all the other clans and, by AD 400, had unified the country under their rule.

According to Japanese legend, Japan was founded in 660 BC by its first emperor, Jimmu, a direct descendant of the sun goddess, Amaterasu. Evidence found in tombs, however, indicates that the first emperors did not begin to reign until sometime after 300 BC. The current emperor, Akihito, descends from a family that is believed to date from the early 500s. This makes his family dynasty the longest-reigning monarchy in the world.

One Race, One People

Two important events that had a profound effect on Japanese history were the halting of various migrations to Japan by the year AD 400 and the expulsion of foreigners from Japan in 1630. Not until the early twentieth century was there any large-scale voluntary

This is the portrait of an Ainu woman with tattooed lips. Traditionally, some Ainu women had their lips tattooed as young girls. The upper lip was cut, and ashes were rubbed into the wound to create a scar.

immigration into Japan. This isolation led to the emergence of a people who were at first both culturally and racially homogeneous for an extremely long time. Despite regional variations and the influx of immigrants from other countries, the Japanese have maintained a fairly unified culture and are almost all members of the Mongoloid race.

Immigration to Japan began about a century ago, when Chinese immigrants who came to work in Japan established their own communities in many of the major port cities. After imperial Japan's colonization of Korea in 1910, migration began between Japan and the Korean peninsula.

Today, aside from the Koreans who make up the largest population of immigrants, there are a few minority groups in Japan. The Ainu, a native people of northern Japan, are one such minority group. At one time their traditional customs and language were banned by the Japanese government. Today, they still remain the targets of racial and cultural discrimination and are among the poorest of Japanese minorities.

Also living in Japan are between 2 and 3 million *burakumin* (which means "helmet people"), who came from the southwest region of Japan. Although this group is considered Japanese, they are thought to be the descendants of

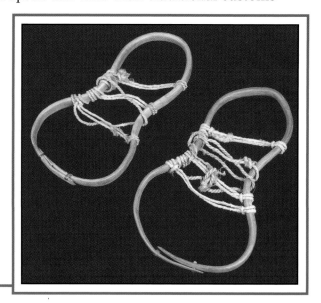

This is a pair of Ainu snowshoes from the early twentieth century. The Ainu have adapted to the cold, harsh winters of northern Japan.

These ancient rock Buddhas at Usuhi, on the island of Kyushu, date from the fifth century AD.

ancient outcasts who once engaged in occupations that were viewed as unclean. These included occupations such as gravediggers, butchers, and leatherworkers. The burakumin also suffer from harsh discrimination and often are found living apart from other Japanese in the slums.

Learning from China

In Japan, under the rule of the Yamato emperors, the court moved frequently from one city to another. At the same time, Japan began drawing on influences from across the sea, first from Korea and later from China. One of the most important developments was the introduction of Buddhism from China in 552. In addition to Buddhism, which in time became the dominant religion of Japan, the Japanese envoys also brought back with them Confucianism and Taoism. The Chinese writing system was also introduced to Japan during this period.

In 645, a series of major changes called the Taika Reforms were carried out. These changes included the creation of a new government and administrative system. This was based in part on the Chinese political system. Under the Taika Reforms, the state bought all land and then redistributed it equally among individual farmers. The redistribution of land paved the way for

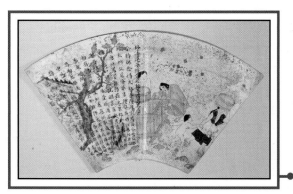

This decorative fan is from the twelfth century AD. It depicts an excerpt from the Lotus Sutra. The Lotus Sutra is an important teaching of Sakyamuni Buddha (Siddhartha Gautama).

A samurai warrior poses with his sword raised for battle in this 1860 photo. In addition to being well-respected as warriors, the samurai were known for their skills in martial arts and education. One samurai saying was "Be both a good warrior and a good scholar."

the creation of a new tax system, also based on Chinese models. With these reforms, Japanese leaders hoped to create a strong central government that gave the emperor almost complete control over his administration and taxation.

However, over time the emperors' authority had diminished. Landowning noblemen, who had inherited high governmental positions, held the real power in Japan. Eventually, these aristocratic landowners did away with the Taika Reforms that had enhanced the power of the emperor. They gradually took more power for themselves.

The Rise of the Shoguns

One consequence of reversing the Taika Reforms was the growth of large private estates known as *shoen*. With the decline of the imperial government, many of these powerful landholders, called *daimyo*, formed vigilante bands of warriors to protect their estates from attack. These warriors, known as *samurai*, were fiercely loyal to the daimyo. In time, the daimyo and their samurai challenged the government for control of Japan, even while they continued to battle each other.

Finally, in 1185, Yoritomo Minamoto defeated his rivals and established a military government. He received the title *shogun*, or supreme military commander, and his government became known as a *shogunate*. Although the Japanese emperor remained on the throne, it was the shogun who ruled the country. For almost 700 years, the shoguns and their samurai ruled Japan.

This sixteenth-century screen depicts the arrival of Portuguese merchants in Japan. The Portuguese brought firearms into Japanese culture. This drastically changed the samurai style of warfare in Japan.

Contact with the West

Before the middle of the sixteenth century, Japan was largely unknown to Europeans. Japan's first contact with the West occurred in 1543, when a Portuguese ship landed off the coast of the southern island of Kyushu. Soon, Japan developed a lively trade with Portugal, Spain, Holland, and England. Jesuit missionaries soon followed in the wake of the Portuguese traders.

Despite the developing commerce with the Portuguese and other Europeans, many Japanese viewed contact with the outside world as a threat to their hard-won peace and way of life. To prevent such external influence, the shoguns began to discourage Christianity, expel the traders, and close Japanese ports to Western vessels. By 1641, only a small number of Dutch and Chinese traders were allowed to do business in Japan. And this was only in the port city of Nagasaki, where the authorities could closely monitor their activities.

An 1853 portrait of Commodore Matthew Perry. After returning from Japan, Perry wrote an account of his expedition entitled, *Narrative of the Expedition of an American Squadron to the China Seas and Japan.*

This Japanese woodblock print shows a demonstration of a U.S. steam locomotive in Yokohama, Japan, in 1854. Prints such as this one were produced to encourage Japanese citizens to accept Western technology.

However, the shoguns' efforts to isolate Japan failed. On July 14, 1853, under the command of Commodore Matthew Perry, a United States Navy squadron entered Edo Bay. Perry had a letter from U.S. president Millard Fillmore demanding that Japan open its ports to American ships and establish trade relations with the United States. On March 31, 1854, the Japanese signed a treaty with the United States, agreeing to open its ports to American commerce. Soon after, European countries made similar treaties with Japan.

The Meiji Restoration and the Rush to Modernize

In 1867, samurai forces from western Japan rose up against the government of the shogun and eventually toppled it. On January 3, 1868, the samurai announced the "restoration" of rule by Emperor Meiji, even though the emperor remained a mere figurehead. The capital city was moved from Kyoto—which had been the Japanese capital from 794 to 1867—to Edo, modern Tokyo.

During the period known as the Meiji Restoration (which lasted until 1912), the Japanese embarked on a program to modernize their country in order to compete with the West. The Meiji reforms included the

This nineteenth-century woodblock print depicts Emperor Mutsuhito holding a council. After the first Sino-Japanese War, Japan gained influence over Korea from the Chinese.

A Japanese military unit awaits command during the Russo-Japanese War. The war began with a surprise attack by the Japanese on Port Arthur on February 8, 1904.

abolition of the feudal system and the adoption of a program of industrialization. The Japanese leaders also created a constitutional government and adopted a Westernized legal system. Other changes abolished the samurai status, replacing it with a more modern, Western-styled army and compulsory military service. A new ruling class began to emerge—the *zaibatsu*. These were families who owned large land estates and large corporations and who also controlled the Japanese economy.

The Push for Empire

Like its European counterparts who were successfully building overseas empires, Japan also wished to expand its borders. As a result, the Japanese engaged in two wars for control of Asian territory. They won both of them: first, against the Chinese in the first Sino-Japanese War of 1894 to 1895, and then against Russia with the Russo-Japanese War of 1904 to 1905.

In 1914, hostilities broke out that eventually led to the First World War (1914–1918). The international conflict pitted most of the nations of Europe along with Russia, the United States, the Middle East, and other regions against the Central powers—Germany, Austria-Hungary, and Turkey. Hoping to win German possessions in eastern Asia, Japan fought against Germany with the victorious Allies. At the 1919 peace conference in Paris, France, Japan was regarded as an equal power to its Western allies.

During the 1920s, Japan began instituting a more democratic system of government. However, the new parliamentary government was not rooted deeply enough to withstand the economic and political pressures of the 1930s, during which military

Soon after the Meiji Restoration in 1868, Western-style newspapers were established. Woodblock prints on local news stories were issued as supplements. In this print from one of Japan's earliest newspapers, the *Yubin hochi shimbun* "Postal Newspaper," a man hurls a rock at his estranged lover.

Hiroshima was utterly destroyed by an atomic bomb in 1945. More than 80,000 people were killed, and an estimated 60,000 died later from nuclear fallout sickness. The bombs dropped on Nagasaki and Hiroshima were the first (and only) atomic weapons to be used offensively.

leaders became increasingly influential. Also during this period, a worldwide economic depression seriously crippled the Japanese economy. With hard times setting in, the growing number of extreme nationalist groups believed that the solution to Japanese problems lay in the expansion of the Japanese empire and the assertion of Japanese power.

World War II

By 1931, relations between Japan and China had reached a breaking point. Earlier, Japan had forced China into a number of unequal economic and political treaties with China's defeat in the Sino-Japanese War. Furthermore, Japan's influence over Manchuria had been steadily growing since the end of the Russo-Japanese War. In

This letter was dropped over cities in Japan after the atomic bomb was dropped by the Americans. The letter warns the Japanese people to evacuate the cities and petition their government to surrender.

THIS IS A WARNING TO THE JAPANESE PEOPLE!
LEAVE THIS CITY IMMEDIATELY!

The contents of this flyer are very important. The Japanese people are facing a very significant change. Your Military rulers were presented the opportunity to stop this pointless war in the Thirteen Articles of the Joint Resolution. Your Military Rulers refused. For this reason the Soviet Union has declared war on Japan. Further, the United States has invented and tested a most formidable weapon, the atomic bomb, even though it was thought impossible. This atomic bomb, alone, is as destructive as the usual bomb load of two-thousand B-29's. (end of first page)

You will know this is true when you have seen the devestation caused by only one atomic bomb dropped on Hiroshima. The Japanese military is causing this pointless war to continue, so we are going to destroy them with this fearsome weapon. Before the United States uses many of these atomic bombs on Japan we wish the Japanese people would petition the Emperor to stop this war.

The President of the United States has announced the Thirteen Articles of the Joint Declaration and hopes the Japanese people will accept these Articles very soon, become a peace loving people and build a new Japan. The Japanese people must stop their military resistance now. If you do not stop this war the United States will be forced to use the atomic bomb and other superior military weapons.

LEAVE THIS CITY IMMEDIATELY!

1931, Chinese nationalists occupied Manchuria in an attempt to push the Japanese out. The Japanese marched into Manchuria and carved from it a puppet state, Manchukuo, where the Manchurian government was controlled by the Japanese. By July 1937, the second Sino-Japanese War had broken out, and soon Japanese forces succeeded in occupying almost the whole coast of China.

By 1940, Japan had aligned itself with the Axis powers, Germany and Italy, who were now at war with the Allied powers of Great Britain and France. Instead of waiting for the United States to declare war on Japan, the Japanese military high command decided to make a defensive strike against the United States. Accordingly, on December 7, 1941, Japan attacked the American Pacific Fleet stationed at Pearl Harbor

Japanese leaders sign a statement of surrender in Hong Kong in 1945. At the end of World War II, Japan lost control of its overseas territories.

A photograph from 1928 shows Japanese emperor Hirohito in England. He ruled Japan from 1926 until 1989. His reign was the longest of all Japanese emperors.

in Hawaii. Soon after, Japan dominated the Pacific. The turning point in the Pacific war came with the Battle of Midway in June 1942, as Allied forces defeated the Japanese navy and slowly won back the territories the Japanese had occupied. On August 6, 1945, the United States dropped an atomic bomb on the city of Hiroshima; three days later, on August 9, another bomb was dropped on the city of Nagasaki. The destruction and devastation of the two bombs was horrific. They completely destroyed the two cities and killed thousands of innocent people. Japan conceded defeat and surrendered. Japan then prepared for occupation by a foreign nation.

Postwar Japan

World War II (1939–1945) devastated Japan. All the large cities (with the exception of Kyoto, which, because of its many cultural treasures, the Americans decided not to bomb), factories, and the transportation networks were severely damaged. Industry was at a standstill. Some 2 million people had died in the war, a third of them civilians. A horrible food shortage continued for several years after the war had ended.

Tokyo's bustling Shinjuku keeps on growing. Shinjuku is full of movie theaters, restaurants, bars, and shops. There is also a large train station in Shinjuku.

A young woman on a subway sends e-mail from her cell phone. The need for constant communication inspires many of Japan's technological innovations.

The Allied occupation of Japan began in August 1945 and ended on April 28, 1952.

By 1955, the Japanese economy was flourishing. Economic growth and prosperity resulted in an improved standard of living. This period also saw the rise of the Liberal Democratic Party (LDP) in Japan. Yet economic growth also forced the Japanese to confront the problems of an industrial society, such as air and water pollution and the depletion of natural resources.

Since the 1970s, Japan has been ruled by moderately conservative governments that have maintained close ties to the West. Parliamentary democracy has become progressively stronger since the 1950s, and the Japanese economy has grown tremendously. By the mid-1990s, Japan was a world leader in every type of industrial production, although a subsequent economic slowdown, a downturn in real estate sales, and a financial crisis have recently troubled the country.

A young couple takes a quiet moment in the Meiji-jingu park, which is in the Shibuya ward of Tokyo.

THE LANGUAGE OF JAPAN

3

A Most Unique Language

The Japanese language is among the most difficult to learn. Yet Japanese ranks as one of the most important languages in the world. More than 130 million people speak Japanese, of which the vast majority—approximately 127 million—live in Japan. Most of the remaining Japanese speakers live in the United States, Canada, Latin America, and Australia—countries where large numbers of Japanese immigrants have settled. Over the last thirty years, there has been a great surge of interest in the study of Japanese in the West. Many Europeans and North Americans have become fascinated with Japanese culture. Because of Japan's growing international influence in business, technology, and commerce, many Westerners have found it necessary to learn Japanese. As a result, special programs in many grade and secondary schools offer instruction in Japanese. Many colleges in a number of Western countries also offer courses in Japanese. Despite its complexity, Japanese currently ranks as one of the most studied languages in the world.

A Language History

There is a great deal of debate among scholars about the origins of the Japanese language. Some experts believe that it is unrelated to any known language. Others suggest

At left, a102-year-old Buddhist priest from Itoman City uses a magnifying glass to read an astrological chart. Above, young Japanese schoolchildren whisper to each other on the morning ride to school. The Tokyo subway is one of the busiest subways in the world. Millions of people ride it everyday.

The large character on the right, Sei (essence), is part of a calligraphic hanging scroll from the Edo period (mid-seventeenth century). The writing was done by a Zen Buddhist monk named Mokuan Shoto. It reads, "Flowers open and heaven reveals its essence."

that Japanese is a mix of languages, borrowing from the Ural-Altaic group that includes Turkish, Mongolian, Manchu, and Korean. In addition, some linguists (scholars who study language) think that Japanese may have borrowed elements from European, Indian, and Chinese sources.

Whatever its origins, Japanese is one of the most unique, complicated, and precise languages in the world. However, it was not until recently that the language gained international influence. In part because of this linguistic isolation from the rest of the world, Japanese has played an important role in unifying the Japanese people. No matter where a person is from in Japan, all speak the same language, though there are some regional dialects.

Speaking Japanese

One reason why Japanese is so difficult to master is the complex patterns of speech it requires. Speaking Japanese demands correct pronunciation and accurate inflection, or tone. Unlike English, in Japanese the wrong tone of voice completely changes the meaning of a word. Moreover, in Japanese, sentences

Students from all over Japan travel to Hiroshima for antiwar protests. At peace rallies, students listen to speeches, raise money for their cause, and wear signs with antiwar messages.

are not composed the same way as they are in English or the Romance languages; instead, the verb always comes at the end of a statement.

A speaker uses different styles of speech to show different levels of familiarity and intimacy. Each of these levels uses different verbs, adjectives, and nouns. The Japanese emphasize politeness in all conversation. Women tend to speak in a more polite style than men. They have even developed an entire system of honorific language, or special grammatical forms used in speaking to or about someone who is socially superior.

Japanese have family names and given names, used in that order. When addressing another person it is common to use –*san*, the equivalent of Mr., Mrs., or Ms. after the family name. For example, a person with the last name of Johnson becomes Johnson-san. The suffix -*chan* is often attached to children's names and the given names of close friends. Other titles, such as *sensei* for "teacher" or "doctor," are also attached as suffixes after the family name.

The Japanese language does not have gender-specific nouns the way that languages such as French, Spanish, or Italian do. In these Romance languages, a word is either male or female in form. Instead, in Japanese, there are some words or phrases that, when spoken, sound distinctly feminine or masculine to native speakers. The Japanese are very careful about their use, because these phrases spoken by the wrong sex would sound ridiculous or even childish.

Even body language is different when speaking Japanese. Sometimes, when talking of oneself, the Japanese point to their noses. When counting with their fingers, they open their hands and bring each finger down to their palm.

Dialects

The rugged, mountainous terrain and the thousands of islands that make up Japan have

A businessman walks in front of a huge television screen broadcasting a speech given by Prime Minister Junichiro Koizumi. On January 31, 2003, Koizumi addressed the Japanese public about the future of Japan's economy.

separated the country into diverse communities, each of which has developed many different dialects or languages. Quite often, speakers of one dialect do not completely understand another dialect. During the twentieth century, however, the influence of radio and television and the implementation of compulsory education have done much to standardize Japanese. Today, most Japanese speak what is known as the Tokyo dialect—the language first spoken by the educated residents of Tokyo.

Japlish

The Japanese have borrowed some English words and created what they call foreign loan words, or Japlish, which adds to the language. Some Japanese believe that as a result of these borrowed words, a new dialect has emerged. According to one language expert, the latest edition of a dictionary of Japlish words contains 43,000 entries. Such publications cannot keep up with the rapidly changing language. These changes may have given rise to some linguistic confusion and uncertainty, but they are also clear signs of a dynamic, living language that has grown neither static nor stale.

A twelfth-century drawing depicts an ancient Japanese calligrapher with ink and rice paper. Calligraphy is a highly respected art form that requires great skill and patience.

Writing Japanese

The Japanese system of writing is as complicated as it is beautiful and elegant. More than 1,500 years ago, the Japanese adopted Chinese characters, called *kanji*, as the basis of their written language. In addition to kanji, the Japanese use two

sets of Japanese syllables called *hiragana* and *katakana*. Hiragana are cursive characters, usually used with kanji to conjugate verbs and create adjectives.

Katakana is used in the same way as hiragana, but it is a print form of writing and is typically used by children or adults when they are first learning to write. The form is also used to describe foreign words. Often, it is also used in conjunction with kanji. Learning kanji is so difficult that it has posed many problems for the Japanese school system. Teaching children to read and write Japanese is a long, slow, and difficult task.

Most Japanese writing is a mixture of kanji and hiragana. Japanese newspapers, magazines, and books are usually printed in columns running from top to bottom which read from right to left. This is the opposite of English, which is read from left to right.

JAPANESE MYTHS AND LEGENDS

4

J apanese myths and legends can be funny, sad, scary, and touching. Many of these stories were created at a time when the world was seen as a very different place, where religion and magic existed side by side. Demons, monsters, and strange creatures were believed to inhabit this world, and the gods had closer contact with humans and often played an important role in their lives. There is a huge variety of characters in Japanese legends, including gods, human heroes, and ghosts.

The myths and legends they inhabit describe how natural occurrences, such as storms or seasons, were created, teach moral lessons, and tell tales that describe early life in Japan. Very early creation legends, warrior and nature tales, ghost stories, and animal legends are also abundant.

The foundation of these Japanese legends comes from two sources. The *Kojiki* (Records of Ancient Matters) was an official Japanese history edited in the year AD 712. These stories were told by an official storyteller, Hieda-no-Arei, and were written down by Oo-no-Yasumaro. The second work is that of the *Nihonshoki* (Chronicles of Japan), which was written at the Japanese imperial court in 720. The *Nihonshoki* consists of thirty volumes of historical narratives that describe the age of the gods through the reign of Empress Jito in the seventh century. The first half of the *Nihonshoki* also contains many myths and legends. Together with the *Kojiki*, the *Nihonshoki* is an important source for the Shinto religion.

At left, a silk scroll depicts Izanami and Izanagi creating the Japanese islands from the sky. Above is a woodblock print of a famous Kabuki character. It depicts the hero, who is stunned to see his beautiful bride magically change into a cat demon, looking away in surprise.

This is a photo of the wedded rocks located at Futamigaura in Ise Bay. According to legend, this is where Izanagi and Izanami created the Japanese islands. The rocks represent the two deities and the sacred union between man and woman.

In both of these collections, many sections of early Japanese history, myths, legends, and songs were written entirely in Chinese, as the Japanese language had not yet been fully developed. When collecting their myths and legends, the Japanese often made concise notes as to when and where certain stories appeared, in order to keep as complete a record as possible. The end result is an amazing array of tales, myths, and legends that are filled with mystery, moral lessons, and a sensitivity to the beauties of the natural world.

Creation Legends

Creation legends are an important part of Japanese mythology. These stories describe the beginnings of the world and Japan, as well as the birth of various gods and goddesses, such as the God of Fire and Thunder or the Goddess of Mercy. According to legend, the universe was not created, but had always existed; stories describe this universe as a misty place. Years passed until, one day, a shapeless mass that was transparent and light rose up from the mist to form the heavens. This became known as the Plain of High Heaven. Its god was known as Ama-no-Minaka-Nushi-no-Kami, or the Deity of the August Center of Heaven. As the legend continues, the heavens gave birth to two gods: Takami-Musubi-no-Kami (the High August-Producing Wondrous Deity) and Kami-Musubi-no-Kami (the Divine-Producing Wondrous Deity). These three divine beings were called the Three Creating Deities. In time, they created more gods—always as male and female pairs.

For a long time, the gods lived in the heavens, where they did very little. Eventually, it was decided that two gods, Izanagi and Izanami, would go to earth. Izanagi was given the gift of a jeweled spear, which he used to dip into the ocean. The drops of water that dripped off his spear became solid. This is how the islands of Japan were created. Later, Izanagi and Izanami married. Their first child, Amaterasu, was a girl of radiant beauty. The gods decided that she was too beautiful to live in Japan, so they placed her in the sky, where she became the sun. The couple had two sons: the first, Susa-No-Wa (the Storm God), was troublesome and the exact opposite of his sister Amaterasu. The second son became the Moon God, Tukuyomi. Other children of the couple grew to become the gods and goddesses of the mountains, trees, rivers, and plains of Japan.

Unfortunately, while giving birth to Kagutsuchi-no-Kami, the deity of fire, Izanami became sick after being burned by the flaming child, and died. This brought death into the world for the first time. Izanami then went to the underworld where all dead souls live. Tormented with grief over the death of his wife, Izanagi followed her there. However, Izanami forbade him to see her. Chasing him away from the underworld, she also punished Izanagi by taking 1,000 lives away from the humans. Izanagi then created 1,500 lives for every thousand Izanami took away. In this way, the islands of Japan were soon filled with people.

According to legends, Ameratsu always suspected that Susanoo secretly envied her powers. Wanting to be safe, she dressed in full armor whenever they met. One day, Susanoo asked her why. Ameratsu told him she did not trust him. Angered, Susanoo destroyed her beautiful garden. Ameratsu then asked Susanoo for his sword, which she then broke. The five pieces of Susanoo's sword fell to the ground and turned in to Ameratsu's five sons: Ameno-Oshihommimi, Ameno-Hohi,

This 1830 woodblock print depicts Okinawa Mara (Little Demon) attacking a giant carp. The scene is from a collection of hero-warrior tales about the famous Benkei.

Amatu-Hikone, Ikutu-Hikone, and Kumano-Kusubi. Later, she performed the same ritual again and created three daughters: Tagiri-Hime, Itukishima-Hime, and Takitu-Hime. The Japanese believe that it is from Ameratsu's daughters that the emperors of Japan descended.

Hero-Warrior Tales

In Japan, hero-warrior tales—another important type of Japanese legend—tell stories of warriors who were strong, skillful, and cunning. These traits helped them outwit their enemies. Many Japanese think of these characters as minor gods.

One of the most famous of Japanese heroes is Saito Musashibo Benkei. Benkei was a historic monk-warrior in feudal Japan. Until the end of the sixteenth century, religious organizations in Japan, such as monasteries, held a great deal of political and military power in addition to their spiritual roles. This allowed monasteries to train troops that helped maintain their power. These warrior-monks were often referred to as *sohei*. Benkei was a loyal servant who also demonstrated great skills and strength as a warrior—all important qualities in Japanese samurai culture. Benkei was also admired for his gentleness and good humor.

In the Japanese hero-warrior tales, Benkei was born the son of a temple official. His appearance—his wild hair and long teeth—frightened people. As a young boy, he was a troublemaker. Ultimately, his exasperated parents sent him to live in a Buddhist monastery. By the age of seventeen, Benkei was over six feet tall and had supernatural strength. He left the monastery and joined the Yamabushi, a sect of wandering bandit monks. As a member of the Yamabushi, Benkei led the life of a

This ink and pigment painting on silk dates from the Edo period. Entitled *Boy on Mount Fuji*, it is by a famous Japanese artist named Hokusai Katsushika.

bandit who would take the sword of each of his victims. In time, Benkei had collected 999 swords.

One evening, when Benkei was ready to take sword number 1,000, a young man by the name of Yoshitsune passed by. He was small and weak-looking and to Benkei's delight, he had a nice sword. Thinking that the young man would be easy to overcome, Benkei surprised Yoshitsune. However, much to his own surprise, Benkei was defeated by his more agile opponent. From that point on, Benkei pledged his life and his sword to Yoshitsune and accompanied him through numerous adventures. The adventure-filled tales of Benkai are very popular with many Japanese children. He embodies many of the qualities that the Japanese still value today: loyalty, humor, and strength.

Nature Tales

Japanese nature tales are stories in which characters such as trees, flowers, and butterflies are possessed with human souls. These tales are based on the Shinto religion, which maintains that nonliving objects, such as trees, rocks, streams, and flowers, are filled with spirits and hold special powers. This helps to explain the great love the Japanese people have for nature. One type of these nature stories can be found in the numerous legends that surround Mount Fuji.

According to the nature stories, Mount Fuji held the secret of eternal life. Unfortunately, for many of the stories' human characters who travel to Fuji, the magic potion is never found. One popular legend tells of a Chinese emperor who, in the company of other travelers, journeyed to Fuji to seek eternal life. As he neared the end of his journey, the emperor ran forward to be the first to taste the potion from the mountain. By the time the rest of travelers caught up with the emperor, he was lying on his back, smiling. He had indeed found eternal life, but only through death.

Many other nature stories explain how certain trees and flowers were created. For instance, one day a Japanese pine tree was making so much noise moving with the wind that the emperor demanded that it be still. The tree was so obedient that from that time on, all Japanese pine trees stood straight and tall and never moved their branches. Another legend explained the strange markings on chestnuts. The Princess Hinako-Nai-Shinno asked that chestnuts be brought for her to eat. However, she ended up eating only one, biting it and then throwing the nut away. The chestnut took root, and from that time on, all chestnuts bore the mark of the Princess's teeth. In this small way, the chestnut showed its devotion to the princess.

Animal Legends

In Japan, animal legends (which are regarded as fairy tales) are quite popular with young children. These stories tend to be lighthearted and humorous. The character of the fox, also known as *kitsune*, is a favorite subject of these tales. In these stories, foxes have the power to change shapes at will, which leads to all kinds of mischief. According to many stories, foxes are best left alone, for they can cause great trouble.

At right is an 1858 drawing depicting the story of *Tamamo-no-Mae* (The Jewel Maiden). Tamamo is a magical fox who takes the shape of a beautiful woman. In Japanese legends, foxes often like to disguise themselves as women in order to trick foolish men.

In the mountainous city of Takayama, a woman gives her dog a drink. The Japanese are fond of household pets—especially dogs and cats.

Tanuki or *ana-gumi* ("raccoon dogs") are also popular characters in Japanese folktales. Like foxes, the tanuki can assume human form and play all sorts of tricks on unsuspecting humans. But tanuki can also be easily tricked and fooled. In Japanese legends, they are very grateful to those who help them. In fact, tanuki often repay humans that do good things for them. Tanuki are often pictured as Buddhist monks, symbolizing gratitude.

Unlike the tanuki, fox, and hare, cats are very unpopular characters in animal legends. This is because, according to legend, the cat and the snake refused to cry when Buddha died. The cat even hunted the rat who had been sent to fetch the medicine to cure the Buddha.

Cats were believed to become *nekomata*, or "goblin cats," unless their tails were cut off. Often endowed with supernatural powers, cats had the ability to bewitch humans. However, Japanese sailors thought very highly of cats—especially those with three colors. It was believed that these cats were able to ward off the spirits of the deep who might sink the ship. In Japan, cats are also believed to have control over the dead spirits of sailors who still live in the sea.

An ancient scroll from the thirteenth century shows a scene of hungry ghosts.

Ghost Stories

Ghost stories have been a mainstay of Japanese culture from their early beginnings in the seventeenth century to today. However, Japanese ghost stories are not meant to scare people, like those in Western cultures. Instead, they are reminders to the Japanese of the "ghostly" or dreamlike reality that is present in everyday life. As a general rule, Japanese ghost stories almost always take place in the summer months. According to Japanese Buddhism, the reason for this is because August is the Bon season, when ancestral spirits are said to return for their annual visit. This summer tradition then creates a perfect backdrop for ghost stories.

Known as Obake, Japanese ghosts often change shapes. For example, a ghost story may describe steam suddenly rising from an umbrella and taking the shape of a hideous face. A bonfire might show the ghostly outline of a person who suddenly disappears. In these stories, as well as many others, the Japanese are reminded that the spirit world exists close to the everyday world of the living.

JAPANESE FESTIVALS AND CEREMONIES OF ANTIQUITY AND TODAY

5

T he Japanese people, who are fond of celebrations, observe fourteen national holidays every year. Most businesses and schools close, and often there are parades complete with fireworks. Besides these national holidays, some Japanese also commemorate important events in the life of the royal family. In addition, there are many festivals, known as *matsuri*. Many cities and villages have their own local festivals to mark various special occasions.

Shogatsu

For the Japanese, the New Year, or Shogatsu, is the most important holiday of the year. Celebrated over three days in January, the New Year is a time for people to make a new start, and this obligation is taken very seriously. In December, people hasten to fulfill all outstanding tasks and duties in order to welcome the coming year with a clean slate. This includes cleaning the house, paying

off old debts, and preparing food for the upcoming celebration. In addition, the

At left, celebrants gather in front of an ice statue of Admiral Matthew Perry at the Sapporo Snow and Ice Festival in Hokkaido. The festival takes place in February, the coldest month in Japan. For the event, the town is decorated with ice and snow sculptures. Above, a man walks on hot coals at the Gengoji Temple during a Buddhist festival.

Japanese adorn the entrances to their homes and their automobiles with special decorations known as *kazari*. Common examples of kazari are arrangements of pine boughs or bamboo grass.

Honoring the Young and the Old

The Japanese also celebrate a number of holidays that honor the young. For example, young girls in Japan eagerly look forward to Doll's Festival or Girl's Day, which is held every year on March 3. This day is special for families with daughters. A girl's first Doll's Festival is called her *hatsu-zekku*. One longstanding tradition requires the girl's grandparents to present her with her first set of *hina* dolls. Every year, many girls also display all the dolls that have been given to them to celebrate Hina-matsuri.

Each year on May 5, Japanese boys celebrate the Boy's Festival Day. But in 1948, the Japanese government changed the celebration to what is now known as the Children's Festival. This day honors all the children of Japan. However, most families celebrate the day as a festival for boys.

A craftsman carefully paints a doll's face. After the dolls' faces are painted, they are attached to cloth bodies. The dolls—known as hina dolls—are typically dressed in elaborate costumes. These dolls are made especially for Girl's Day.

On this day, families with sons fly carp streamers, or *koi nobori*, outside their houses. The streamers are usually made of paper or cloth and are hung on tall bamboo or wooden poles that are placed in the yard or garden. The carp is an important symbol to the Japanese. It signifies strength, determination, and energy.

On November 15, young boys and girls celebrate Shichi-go-san, or 7-5-3. This special occasion is for boys aged three and five and girls aged three and seven. Parents take their children to a local shrine to give thanks for their health and to pray for their future. Children especially look forward to a special treat of "thousand-year candy," or *chitose-ame*. The red-and-white candy stick, which measures almost a foot long (31 cm), comes in big bags, and is sweet and crunchy.

Golden Week and Other Holidays

In Japan, April 29 through May 5 is Golden Week. This is a busy time when three national holidays are celebrated in succession. Many people take time off from work and school for the entire week to celebrate. The week begins with Greenery Day on April 29 to honor the late Emperor Showa's great love of nature. On May 3, the Japanese celebrate Constitution Memorial Day, which commemorates the creation of the Japanese government after World War II and the Japanese constitution, which was also adopted on this day. The week ends with Children's Day on May 5.

Other national celebrations in Japan include cherry blossom viewing. Called Hanami, or "flower viewing parties," these are annual springtime events in which people travel to experience the colorful burst of cherry blossoms. No matter where one goes, there are cherry

In Hiroshima on the fiftieth anniversary of the atomic bombing, lanterns were placed on the river to remember the victims. Every year on August 6, the city holds a peace memorial, where people come to pray for those who lost their lives and to advocate peace.

In Yamanashi, young children celebrate Setsubun by dressing up as demons. The children compete in a beanbag toss and win prizes. Setsubun is celebrated differently throughout Japan. Each region or city has its own traditions.

trees to be seen. Daily reports on radio and television alert people to the best sites for viewing. People drink, eat, and sing during the day and night.

Around February 4, Setsubun, the Bean-Throwing Festival, is celebrated. This marks the beginning of spring. On the night of Setsubun, a *mame-maki*, or bean-throwing ceremony, is held. A square wooden measuring cup, known as a *masu*, is filled with roasted soybeans. The beans are then thrown all over the room, as people shout, "Oni wa soto! Fuku wa uchi!" ("Out with the devils and in with good fortune!"). Windows are opened and beans are also thrown outside.

Between August 13 and 16, the Japanese hold the Bon Festival or All Soul's ceremonies. Families welcome back the souls of their ancestors for a day. To guide the souls back home, a small bonfire is lit outside the house, called a *mukae-bi*, or "welcoming flame." When Bon ends, the spirits are sent off with another bonfire, called *okuri-bi*. In some regions, small lanterns are lit with candles. These are floated down rivers or into the sea as part of the okuri-bi ritual.

During Namahage, two participants dressed as demons hunt for lazy children. This tradition is one way the Japanese teach their children about the importance of hard work.

Regional and City Celebrations

In addition to national holidays, a number of local and regional festivals are celebrated in Japan. Gion Matsuri is an annual festival held in Kyoto. It is one of the three biggest local festivals in Japan. Held throughout the month of July, the highlight of the celebration takes place on July 17, when thirty-two colorful floats, known as Yamaboko-junka, form a long procession and are pulled through the main streets of Kyoto.

Namahage is one of the most unusual festivals in Japan. It takes place every year on January 15 and is celebrated in the Oga Peninsula of Akita Prefecture. The festival celebrates a Japanese legend in which the Namahage gods visit villages on New Year's Day. Young bachelors dress as the Namahage wearing demon masks, straw raincoats, and shoes. They visit each home in a village and ask if there are any disobedient or lazy children who live there. The purpose of this visit is to remind children to be good all year round.

THE RELIGIONS OF JAPAN THROUGHOUT ITS HISTORY

6

Compared to other nations that have state religions—where the majority of people practice a specific religion—most contemporary Japanese are not members of any formal religion. Yet many Japanese people believe firmly in Confucianism. This is a Chinese philosophy created by a little-known schoolteacher who lived in the sixth and seventh centuries and created rules for good behavior.

However, mixed in with the teachings of Confucius are Buddhist and Shinto beliefs. It is not uncommon for many Japanese to practice various religions. For instance, on New Year's Day, a person who visits a Shinto shrine to offer prayers for the New Year may celebrate his or her wedding with a Christian ceremony and may later have funeral services at a Buddhist temple. Because Confucianism, Shintoism, and Buddhism focus on different viewpoints, most Japanese have no trouble following all three beliefs and practices.

Shinto

The Shinto religion, which dates back to the prehistoric ages, is known as the way of the gods. Apart from being the oldest religion in Japan, Shintoism is also the only religion to originate there. Shintoism is based on the worship of millions of spirits

At left is the Itsukushima Shinto shrine, located on the tidal flats of Miyajima Island, which is just off the coast of Hiroshima. Built during the thirteenth century, the shrine is often visited by Japanese and tourists alike. Above, Shinto priests leave their ceremonial shoes at the entrance of the Taisha Shinto shrine.

in the natural world, called *kami*. The kami include such spirits as the creator, the moon, stars, mountains, rivers, waterfalls, seas, winds, fire, and some animals. Shintoists also worship their ancestors. Shintoism does not have a founder, nor does it have sacred scriptures like the Sutras, which are the religious texts of the Hindus.

The Shinto religion was most prominent from the sixteenth to the nineteenth centuries. This was due in part to the adoption of Shintoism as a state religion under the imperial rule of the Meiji Restoration. Because Shintoism received official state support, many Japanese viewed it not just as a religion, but as a way to celebrate Japanese patriotism. By the 1930s, Japanese nationalists and militarists who came to power adapted Shintoism for their own purposes in the hopes of establishing an empire throughout eastern Asia. However, by the end of World War II, Shintoism as a state religion was abolished by the U.S. military authorities.

Today, Shintoism plays a much smaller role in the lives of the Japanese people. Still, numerous shrines are visited regularly by believers and, if they are famous, by tourists. Many marriages are held in the shrines. Often, children are brought to the shrines after birth and on certain anniversary dates; special shrine days are celebrated for specific occasions, and numerous festivals are held throughout the year.

In contrast to followers of other world religions, Shintoists do not believe in absolutes. This means that Shintoists do not have fixed ideas of what is right and what is wrong. Shintoists also believe that no one is perfect. The Shinto religion is a hopeful faith; people are thought to be basically good, and evil is believed to be caused by evil spirits.

Shinto shrines are the places of worship and the homes of kami. Sacred objects of worship that represent the kami are stored in the innermost chamber of each shrine, where they cannot be seen by anybody. No matter where the shrine is located, there are usually certain structures and objects that are typically found within. These include the *torii*, an entrance gate which is usually nothing more than two crossbeams of wood (or stone, concrete, or bronze) resting on two vertical posts. The gates stand about 10 feet (3 m) tall and are usually made of wood. Often, they are painted orange and black, or red. Sometimes, *komainu*, which can be either a pair of guardian dogs or lions, are found on either side of the torii. Purification troughs are located at the entrance; people clean their hands as a kind of symbolic cleansing before entering the shrine.

Each shrine has a main hall, or *honden*, and an offering hall, called a *haiden*. The main hall and offering hall can often be found in one building, though sometimes there are separate buildings for each. The main hall's innermost chamber contains the shrine's sacred object; this is where visitors make their prayers. In many cases, visitors write their wishes on *ema*, or small wooden boards, which are left at the shrine. Offerings made to the various gods are given in the haiden. In addition to the honden and the haiden, there are sometimes other buildings at a Shinto shrine. These may include the priest's house and office, a storehouse for *mikoshi* (small, portable shrines), and other auxiliary buildings. Cemeteries, on the other hand, are almost never found at shrines. The emphasis in the Shinto religion is on everyday life and the community, and death is considered to be an impurity.

The grounds of a Shinto shrine also play a part in religious observances. Trees surrounding the shrine are often covered with *omikuji*, or fortune-telling paper slips, which contain predictions ranging from *daikichi* (great good luck) to *daikyo* (great bad luck). By tying the piece of paper around the branch of a tree, good fortune will come true or bad fortune can be averted. *Shimenawa* is a straw rope with white zigzag paper strips called *gohei*. These ropes mark the boundary to something sacred. They are often found on torii gates, around sacred trees and stones.

Confucianism

Confucianism is not a religion but a system of beliefs for social relationships. It originated in China during the sixth century BC, through the ideas of Confucius, who was a great teacher in China. He believed that by pursuing his teachings, people could improve themselves and

At Inari Taisha, a Shinto priest watches over businessmen who bow before the shrine. At Inari Taisha, businessmen come to pray for their success.

In Izumo, paper prayers are placed at the base of a tree at the Oyashimo shrine. Worshippers write down their prayers and stick them into the ground with pins. The Oyashimo shrine is dedicated to the kami who signifies family and love.

their communities. This philosophy was introduced into Japan from Korea around AD 285. Confucianism was adopted primarily by the ruling elite.

Under Confucianism, people were seen as bound to one another by *jin*, or human kindness. For relationships to be in harmony, one must follow *rei*, which combines both etiquette and ritual. According to Confucius, a person may be superior to some people and inferior to others. But no matter his or her place in society, one must treat all people with kindness and good manners. In particular, the philosophy emphasized respect toward one's elders and to people in positions of authority.

Confucianism has two goals: to develop compassion and respect for other people and to prepare individuals for government service. If government officials follow Confucius's teachings, not only will there be a good government, but a peaceful society filled with content people. Overseeing this society would be a leader who sets the

The world's largest *shimenawa* hangs in Japan's oldest Shinto shrine in Izumo. Shimenawa are rice and straw ropes that symbolize holiness and sacredness.

moral example for the state and who must, at all times, be virtuous and honorable to his people. Today, although most Japanese are not Confucian at all, Japanese manners, beliefs, and social behavior are still profoundly influenced by the doctrine.

Buddhism

The Buddhist religion originated in India and was introduced into Japan from Korea in the sixth century. Even though many Japanese already observed the Shinto religion, most felt no conflict between both faiths. This was because many Japanese believed the kami spirits were linked to the Buddhist gods.

Buddhism played a very important role in early Japanese history, especially in training samurai warriors. According to the Buddhist teaching, for a person to be happy in life, he or she must first overcome selfishness and the need for material things. Buddhists also believe that life continues after death.

Today, there are six major schools of Buddhism in Japan. These include the Tendai school, which emphasizes scholarly and philosophical thought. At the Tendai temples on Mount Hiei near Kyoto, a number of priests devote themselves to pursuits such as studying and writing. The Shingon school practices magical formulas, which not only promise salvation but also worldly gain. Shingon mysticism has greatly influenced the practices of all Buddhist sects. The Jodo school teaches that because man is sinful, he cannot achieve salvation through his own efforts. Instead, he must do so through the merciful compassion of the Amida Buddha. According to the teachings, Amida Buddha was once king of a country hundreds of years ago.

This photo shows student monks who are chanting Sutras (prayers) in front of a lantern. This lantern is symbolic of the guiding light of Shingon. Shingon was founded in AD 816 by a monk named Kukai. He is also known as Kobo-Daishi.

Having heard of the teachings of Buddha, he gave up his throne and began a spiritual journey. To many, Amida Buddha is the embodiment of enlightenment, compassion, and wisdom. It is he alone who decides a person's destiny.

One of the most well-known Buddhist philosophies, Zen Buddhism, is one of the larger and more popular religious groups in Japan. Zen Buddhism has a long historic tradition. It has influenced many aspects of Japanese society, from samurai warriors to Japanese painters and artists. Zen Buddhism emphasizes self-discipline, meditation, and rigor as the way to enlightenment.

New Religions

The largest religious group in Japan today is Soka Gakkai. Established in 1930 by Makiguchi Tsunesaburo, Soka Gakkai strives to improve the world through the practice of Nichiren Buddhism. There are approximately 8.2 million Japanese families

who practice Soka Gakkai. The religion is also finding a larger audience worldwide. The group is active politically and supports the Kemeito "Clean Government" Party, established by Soka Gakkai members. This is considered to be one of the most powerful political groups of the Japanese coalition government.

The Kamakura Buddha was built in 1252. The statue was originally the center-piece in Kotokuin Temple. However, in 1369, the temple was destroyed in a storm, leaving only the Kamakura Buddha standing.

There are also a number of other new religions that can be observed in Japan. Many of these groups were formed in response to the modern problems of everyday life in Japan, especially those resulting from increased urbanization, industrialization, and changes in traditional roles and responsibilities. The majority of these new religions are little more than large social fraternities that appeal to the least educated in Japanese society. Their ceremonies, often highly emotional and filled with references drawn from other religious sources, frequently promise miracle healing.

Many of these new groups make use of new technology, such as audiovisual materials or videotapes, to attract members. They also make use of popular formats, such as comic books or *manga*, which outline the teachings of a particular group or describe the life of the religion's founder. Some of the larger groups produce videotaped rituals or ceremonies, television programs, and even animated films to reach potential members.

Christianity

In 1542, the first Europeans from Portugal landed on Kyushu in western Japan, bringing with them gunpowder and Roman Catholicism. The Japanese shoguns were more interested in the new weaponry and merely tolerated the Jesuit missionaries who accompanied the traders. The Jesuits successfully converted quite a large number of people in western Japan to Catholicism, including members of the ruling class.

By the end of the sixteenth century, a number of Franciscan missionaries arrived in Kyoto, despite a proclamation banning Christian missionaries by the shogun Tokugawa Ieyasu. The shogun and his successors continued the persecution of Christians throughout Japan for many years. By 1638, Christianity was almost extinct. However, a small group of believers hid and survived. After the Meiji Restoration in 1868, freedom of religion was again granted, and missionaries representing many different Christian faiths once again came to Japan.

Since World War II, the number of Japanese Christians has increased. Today, about 1 to 2 million, or approximately 1 percent, of the Japanese population are Christians. Many live in western Japan, where early

This sixteenth-century painting depicts Saint Francis Xavier with his followers. Saint Francis is said to have converted many people to Christianity.

During an Easter vigil, Catholics attend Mass in Nagasaki. Women and men sit on opposite sides of the church. Missionaries who live in Japan spread Christianity throughout small communities and large cities.

missionaries' activities were the greatest. Several Christian holidays and rituals have also become popular among all Japanese, including celebrating Christmas and wearing white dresses at weddings.

Islam

The Islamic religion is a relative newcomer to Japan. While the teachings of Islam were available as early as 1877, when Japanese translations of Islamic works were made, the religion did not attract many converts. As a result, the real Muslim community in Japan did not appear until around 1917. At this time, several hundred Turkoman, Uzbek, Tajik, Kirghiz, Kazakh, and other Turko-Tatar Muslim refugees from central Asia and Russia escaped the Bolshevik Revolution in Russia. These Muslims were given asylum in Japan, where they settled in several main cities and formed small Muslim communities. A number of Japanese converted to Islam through contact with these Muslims. Another result of these Muslim communities is that several mosques have been built. The most important of them is the Kobe Mosque, built in 1935.

THE ART AND ARCHITECTURE OF JAPAN

7

A s with other aspects of their culture, with art and architecture, the Japanese absorbed, imitated, and assimilated various foreign techniques and styles that complemented their own preferences. Japanese art and architecture remain unique in their beauty, philosophy, method, and materials. These works include paintings and sculptures as well as pottery, porcelain, lacquerware, textiles, and woodcuts. All of these art forms are considered traditional in the sense that the artist relies on the use of natural materials to make them.

No matter the medium, Japanese art has always been held in extremely high esteem. This is not only because of its simplicity, but also for its colorful exuberance. The Japanese arts have also influenced the arts in the West. Both European and American artists have been fascinated by Japanese art and incorporated many artistic techniques from Japanese prints. These artists were attracted to the strong sense of design and pattern found in Japanese art as well as the use of bright and harmonious colors.

Calligraphy

Calligraphy is the demanding art of turning ordinary handwriting into a beautiful form. Buddhist monks, both Chinese and Japanese, introduced calligraphy into

At left, a craftsman delicately paints a design onto a silk kimono. Kimonos have been worn in Japan since the eleventh century AD. Above is a collection of colorful origami animals. Origami figures range from simple to complex. Some origami designs require multiple pieces of paper and thousands of tiny, precise folds.

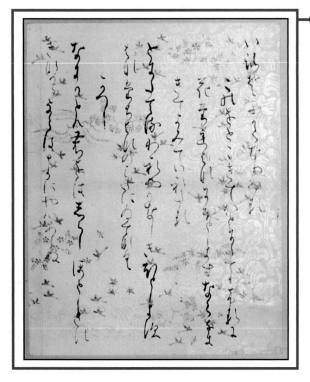

This is a twelfth-century poem written in calligraphy. Calligraphic artistry enhances the beauty of the poetry. Most ancient Japanese poems were carefully written with great flair.

Japan. Among the first practitioners were Zen Buddhist priests. In time, the Japanese departed from Chinese calligraphic patterns and created their own style using Japanese letters known as hiragana. This became the most distinctive Japanese type of calligraphy. However, the use of Chinese characters continued. In the writing style of hiragana, letters are written together without a break, and spacing plays a large role. In other styles, the calligrapher may combine hiragana and kanji, or use only kanji.

Painting

Painting is the preferred artistic expression in Japan. It is popular because until modern times the Japanese wrote with a brush rather than a pen. As a result, they became very familiar with brush techniques that could easily be adapted to painting. Like many other Japanese art forms, early Japanese painting was heavily influenced by Chinese culture.

Classical Japanese painting, or *suibokuga* (ink and water), uses black ink called *sumi*, which is made by mixing the soot of burning pine twigs

This ink painting shows a Japanese landscape. Both broad and fine brushstrokes are used to achieve depth, tonality, and shadowing effects.

This silk hanging scroll illustrates Jioin Daishi, the founder and patriarch of the Hosso sect of Buddhism. This painting dates back to the eleventh century.

with resin to produce a long flat-sided ink stick. The artist then dips the stick into a small pool of water on a flat inkstone and mixes it until the desired shade of ink is achieved.

The material used to paint on was tissue-thin silk, or *washi*. Washi is a Japanese paper that is hand-molded from the fibers of plants such as kozo and mulberry. Washi is remarkably durable and has been known to last 1,000 years.

The Chinese influence remained strong in Japanese painting until the beginning of the Edo period (1603–1867). Although Japanese paintings during this time were often realistic—they depicted nature or daily life in Japan—they were also highly stylized. This means that the images were not painted as they really appeared. These were often called studio pictures. This is because they were created in the artist's workspace, and the artist worked from his imagination and memory.

Woodblock Prints

Woodblock prints were made in Japan as early as the eleventh century. The process was relatively simple. An image

A craftsman makes washi (rice paper) at a workshop. Washi became popular during the Heian period when the royal court needed paper for official documents and personal writing such as diaries and poetry.

This woodblock print by famous artist Ando Hiroshige is called *The Hill by the Lake*. It is part of a very beautiful series of prints named 53 Stages of the Tokaido. Mount Fuji can be seen on the left.

was carved into a piece of wood, usually cherry wood. The carved woodblock was next covered with ink and then pressed to a sheet of paper. The printed image on the paper is known as a woodblock print.

The process of making the prints relied on the skills of several artists and artisans. One artist painted the picture, another carved the image into the woodblock, while others made the paper, mixed the inks, painted the inks on the woodblocks, and printed the block. Two of the most celebrated woodblock artists were Katsushika Hokusai (1760–1849) and Ando Hiroshige (1797–1858), who created one of the most famous woodblock print series, 36 Views of Mt. Fuji.

Sculpture

In general, the Japanese are not as fond of sculpture as they are of painting or woodblock prints. Early Japanese sculptures were associated with religion. The

This style of sculpture is known as Haniwa. Sculptures like this one were placed in mausoleums along with noble people during burial proceedings.

introduction of Buddhism to Japan in the sixth century influenced the development of sculptural techniques, styles, and subjects. For instance, between the sixth and eighth centuries, temple sculptures of the Buddha and other gods were often made of gilt, or gold-covered bronze. One of the most impressive gilt statues from this period is a 52-foot (16 m) seated Buddha in the Todaiji, a very famous temple in the city of Nara (near Kyoto). As the importance of Buddhism declined, however, so did the use of sculpture.

The majority of Japanese sculpture was made of clay or wood. While stone sculptures were not as common, Jizo, the Buddhist god of children, is made of stone. One example of clay sculpture is the *haniwa*, or clay cylinders, that date from the third to the fifth centuries. Elaborate images of animals, birds, and human figures were impressed into clay. By the ninth century, Japanese artists were sculpting figures primarily from wood, which was then plentiful throughout the country.

A statue of Jizo stands in a crowded children's cemetery in Hiroshima. Jizo is a bodhisattva (Buddhist savior). Statues of Jizo are often placed beside the graves of those who died young.

Today, Japanese sculptors continue to look to nature and the Shinto religious tradition, among others, for their inspiration. The sculptors use organic materials, including wood, stone, and fibers, to depict the natural process of life in growth and decay.

Decorative Arts

In Japan, the decorative arts—which are an important part of Japanese art history—include pottery, ceramics, textiles, and lacquerware. The decorative arts were generally created by people who were not professional artists. However, today, both professional and amateur artists are involved in making these different types of decorative art forms.

Japan has one of the oldest ceramic traditions in the world, dating back to 10,000 BC, when the first clay pottery, called jomon, or "cord-marked" pottery, appeared. Until the seventeenth century, all Japanese ceramics were created out of earthenware, a reddish, non-waterproof clay that is fired at low temperatures, or stoneware, a harder clay fired at high temperatures and then glazed. The popularity of tea drinking and the tea ceremony—an elaborate ritual to prepare and drink tea—spurred the growth of ceramic production in Japan. People became concerned with looking for a variety of teaware, such as cups and teapots in different shapes, sizes, and colors.

Lacquerware consists of highly varnished household accessories, such as trays, tables, small chests, containers for tea leaves and candy, and elaborate picnic boxes. Lacquer was carefully applied to a prepared base made from wood, metal, or paper. Red and black were the most common colors for Japanese lacquerware. Sometimes gold and silver metal dust were sprinkled onto still-wet lacquer, giving the piece an even richer look. At present, there are many regions and towns in Japan that are noted for their skillful creations of lacquerware.

This is a collection of gold and red lacquered Japanese boxes. Lacquered boxes are often used to hold medicine and small pieces of jewelry.

A master weaver, Fujita Sentaro patiently and carefully designs intricate scenes on a silk sash. Woven scarves are very expensive items because of the skill and immense amount of time that go into making them.

Origami

Another popular art form is origami, the art of paper folding. Origami was brought to Japan from China by Buddhist monks in the first century AD. The art form was used in a practical manner as the Chinese made vases, bowls, and boxes from folded paper. The Japanese quickly integrated the practice into everyday life. Paper-folding techniques were passed from generation to generation by mothers and daughters. No matter how intricate the final design, origami still follows the original concept that the piece must be made exclusively by folding paper—no glue, tape, staples, or scissors can be used.

Ikebana and Bonsai

Being in harmony with nature is very important to the Japanese. Not only is nature seen as beautiful, but it provides important lessons in life. For example, the Japanese believe that man lives within the order of nature. In daily life, the Japanese surround themselves and interact with nature. One example is the art of raising bonsai, or dwarfed potted trees. This allowed people to appreciate nature in an indoor setting.

Another means of enjoying nature in the home is through the arrangement of flowers, which the Japanese have refined into an art known as ikebana. This means "flowers kept alive." Unlike Western floral arrangements, which emphasize the color and form of flowers, ikebana favors the flowing lines of stems, leaves, and branches.

An ikebana artist carefully places some blossoms into a vase. Flower arrangements are considered to be carefully and skillfully balanced works of art. Some students study the art form their whole lives.

Architecture

As with traditional Japanese painting and sculpture, Japanese architecture made its greatest advances following the introduction of Buddhism. Wood was the primary material used in building. The design of traditional Japanese architecture emphasized horizontal lines. Even in taller structures, such as pagodas, the use of sloping roofs helps minimize the impression of height. Temples, monasteries, and castles are the major architectural monuments. Japan has also produced a number of noteworthy contemporary buildings. In fact, Japan is considered a worldwide architectural design leader. In addition to the built landscape, the Japanese also have created unique landscape garden design, another expression of artistry.

Temples

The oldest buildings in Japan are religious temples and shrines. The designs of these buildings owe much to Chinese influences—in particular, the addition of many-storied pagodas and flared tile roofs. A feature of many temples

The Golden Pavilion is located on the banks of the sparkling Kyoko Pond in Kyoto. The original building was built in 1397 but has since been destroyed and rebuilt three times.

is the exposed timber beams and bracket system that holds the timber beams together without nails. Later temples, such as those built during the thirteenth century, may have additional halls, Sutra repositories, and a refectory. The central gate (*chumon*) has a heavy roof that is similar to that of the buildings. The gate contains sculptures of guardian deities.

There are a number of outstanding examples of temple architecture in Japan, including Rohuon-ji, or the Golden Pavilion, in Kyoto. Built in the eleventh century, it was originally a nobleman's villa. Its shape suggests a phoenix (a mythical bird). The stately structure's reflection can be seen in the pond near which it stands. Japan is also home to the oldest temple and oldest wooden building in the world, the Horyu-ji in Nara, which was constructed in about 607.

Shinto shrines are built in the style of prehistoric storehouses, which were simple wood buildings raised off the ground on piers. Made of untreated wood that weathers over time, the boards can easily be replaced and the entire shrine can be rebuilt when necessary. Shinto shrines are routinely demolished as part of a purification ritual. This usually occurs every twenty or thirty years. A new building is then built, which replicates the earlier structure.

Castles

Many castles were built in Japan in the sixteenth century, when the samurai spirit dominated Japanese society. Though originally built as military defenses, castles also fulfilled an important peacetime role

The impressive Osaka Castle towers over nearby trees. The castle is more than 400 years old. Today, it symbolizes the rich history and traditions of the people of Osaka.

From the windows of a top-floor apartment, one can view the towering skyline of Tokyo on a clear spring day. Tokyo is the most populated metropolis in the world. Because space is limited, apartment high-rises (as opposed to houses) are common homes for many residents.

as the symbol of a lord's prestige and the center of administration. For this reason, they were designed not only for military purposes, but also with aesthetics in mind.

Many Japanese cities began as castle towns that were built as the result of the civil wars of the fifteenth and sixteenth centuries. Surrounded by walls and moats, they were made of stone and wood, complete with many roofs and towers. Solid yet elegant, these castles are characterized by their pagoda-styled roofs, another influence of Chinese architecture. Today there are approximately thirty-seven castles in Japan.

Modern Architecture

The Meiji Restoration in 1868 introduced modern architectural techniques such as the use of brick and gaslighting to Japan. Office buildings and residences incorporating Western designs became increasingly common. In addition, stone and brick structures built by conventional methods failed to stand up to the numerous earthquakes that plagued the country.

Building earthquake-resistant structures has posed a constant challenge, but with the introduction of earthquake technology, such as reinforced concrete, the Japanese built their first skyscraper in 1968—the Kasumigaseki Building. A number of large-scale housing projects, such as Osaka's Senri New Town, have sprung up to meet the demand for housing brought on by increases in the country's population. Japanese architecture continues to test the boundaries of design and building technology, as seen in the urban redevelopment projects in central Tokyo and the introduction of "smart buildings" like the Ark Hills and Yebisu Garden Place complexes. These "cities within a city" consist of several buildings and skyscrapers, and they are connected to the world's most advanced telecommunications networks.

Gardens

At one time, almost every Japanese house maintained some type of garden. These gardens were simple, yet elegantly and gracefully designed. While there was no one way to construct a garden, most every garden contained standard elements such as moss, which creates texture, and stone lanterns, which add a sense of tradition. The clean and simple lines of sand, rock, and stone in Zen gardens provided a place for quiet reflection, contemplation, and prayer. Small structures, such as bridges, or ponds filled with brightly colored koi were reminders for the owner to enjoy the small things in life that were so easily overlooked. However, in today's Japan, this is no longer true. Space is becoming more and more limited, especially in cities. These days, some of the best examples of Japanese gardens can be found on temple grounds.

Koumyouzenji Temple is located in the Fukuoka Prefecture on the island of Kyushu. The temple is one of the oldest in the Buddhist Rinzaishu sect. The temple's rock garden is famous around the world for its beauty and intricate design.

THE LITERATURE AND MUSIC OF JAPAN

8

The Japanese enjoy a rich and diverse literary tradition. Japanese literature, which consists of fiction, poetry, essays, and drama, traces its beginnings to the early legends and stories that were recorded in written form in the early eighth century after the Chinese writing system was introduced. Poetry in particular plays an important role in Japanese culture. Special occasions, such as birthdays, are celebrated with poems. And each year, thousands of poems are submitted for an annual poetry prize that is awarded by the emperor on New Year's Day.

Japanese theater also enjoys a long history. Traditional Japanese theater is but one of many art forms that the Japanese government helps pay for. This ensures that all Japanese have the opportunity to see Japanese theater performances both on stage and on television.

Poetry

Japanese poems, which usually do not rhyme, are based on a syllable count. The first Japanese history, written around AD 712, is one of the earliest examples of Japanese poetry. Early Japanese poetry was written in the style known as *tanka*, or "short form." Tanka poetry consists of thirty-one syllables, arranged in five lines, with

At left, an actor paints his face before going on stage to play a character called Kagekiyo in a Kabuki theater. Kabuki theater was founded in 1603 by an attendant at the Izumo Shrine in Kyoto. Above is a photograph of Japanese actor and director Kitano Takeshi. He has directed eleven movies and performed in more than thirty roles in film and television.

This is an eighteenth-century *surimono* ("printed thing"). Surimono were valuable paintings that featured haikus. They were typically given as gifts on New Year's.

five syllables in the first line, seven in the second, and five in the third. The remaining two lines consist of seven syllables each. Up until the sixteenth century, nearly all poetry was written in the tanka form.

Over time, another form of poetry emerged—the *renga*, or "linked poem." This consists of the same structure as the tanka. The difference with the renga is that two or more poets must work on the same poem. The first poet composes the opening lines, and the second poet finishes the renga. Another popular type of poetry is the *haiku* or "opening phrase." Haiku poetry usually describes a single image and is almost always based on nature. One rule of haiku poetry is that each verse must contain seventeen syllables and be made up of three lines. The first line is five syllables, the second line is seven syllables, and the third line is five syllables.

Other forms of Japanese poetry include the *senryu*, a limerick or humorous rhyming verse, and the acrostic, where the poet creates a poem in verse. In this type of poem, the first or last letters of each line form a word or phrase when read as a line. Modern Japanese poetry, while drawing on traditional influences, also borrows from Western poetic forms that include longer verses or more "free-form" verses where no rules are observed in writing the poem.

This calligraphy, called Waka-shikishi, (a type of haiku done on thick paper), was done by Koetsu and Sotatsu around the seventeenth century. It features a haiku and a flock of cranes.

Prose

Early Japanese literature was written in Chinese. These accounts, written only by men, consisted of essays and official histories written for the court of the emperor. But with the introduction of hana, many Japanese women began contributing to Japan's literature. For instance, in the eighth century women wrote two of Japan's most important works. These were the *Kojiri* (Records of Ancient Matters) and the *Nihonshoki* (Chronicles of Japan). Both of these collections contain not only history, but myths, legends, and songs. By the tenth century, the use of Chinese began to decline. In its place, a unique form of Japanese literature emerged using the newly developed letters of the Japanese language. In general, this early Japanese literature tended to be stories that were a series of loosely connected episodes, much like a diary.

During the period from the ninth to the twelfth centuries, the majority of prose was written by Japanese women, as many Japanese men thought writing was beneath them and viewed it as little more than a source of court gossip. One of the greatest works in Japanese literature, *The Tale of Genji*—an episodic novel from the beginning of the eleventh century—was written by a woman named Shikibu Murasaki. Murasaki was a writer in residence at the Japanese court around the year 1000. An instant success, *The Tale of Genji* exerted wide influence over Japanese literature for centuries.

With the arrival of the United States naval fleet under the command of Commodore Matthew C. Perry in 1853, Japanese literature underwent a dramatic change. When translations of European works began to appear in Japan, Japanese writers discovered that Western literature had different qualities. Among these differences was the use of realism, including the use of everyday language by common

This is an illustration from *The Tale of Genji*, written by Shikibu Murasaki. Murasaki was a lady-in-waiting to the empress of Japan. *The Tale of Genji* remains a classic love story to this day.

This is a photograph of author Yukio Mishima in 1966. Mishima wrote more than forty novels, poems, and essays. He also wrote a few dramas for Kabuki and Noh theater. He was nominated for the Nobel Prize for Literature three times. A famous nationalist, he killed himself.

people, instead of the formal and flowery language of the Japanese royal court.

Since that time, Japanese literature has found a new worldwide audience. One of Japan's greatest writers was Natsume Soseki (1867–1916). Soskei, whose real name was Natsume Kinnosuke, became popular for his work *I Am a Cat*, which was originally published in installments during the years 1904 to 1906. It was translated in 1961. The book describes the adventures of a world-weary cat during the Mejii era. The character of the cat was used by Soseki to make observations about Japanese upper-middle-class society.

Several other Japanese writers have won important awards. This has drawn even more international readers to Japanese literature. In 1968, Yasunari Kawabata became the first Japanese to win the Nobel Prize for Literature; Oe Kenzaburo won it in 1994. In addition, they and other contemporary writers, such as Junichiro Tanizaki, Yukio Mishima, Kobo Abe, and Inoue Yasushi, have been translated into many languages. In the last few years, works by Ryu Murakami, Haruki Murakami, Banana Yoshimoto, and others have also been widely translated. These writers have gained tremendous popularity with audiences throughout the world.

Manga

Manga—cartoon stories published as books or magazines—are tremendously popular in Japan with both adults and children. Some stories continue from one issue to the next. Manga first became popular during the post–World War II years. At this time, artists sought to re-create the drama and action of the movie screen in a cheaper, simpler form. Over the years, these comics have evolved into a multibillion-dollar industry in Japan.

The roots of manga lie in Buddhist scrolls of the sixth and seventh centuries that depict life after death. The earliest manga were printed using wood blocks and paper.

At right is a poster from *Inu-Yasha: A Feudal Fairy Tale,* a manga book by Rumino Takahashi. It details the adventures of a modern Japanese schoolgirl named Kagome, who is magically transported to feudal Japan.

By the 1600s, Japan's merchant class was growing richer and had developed an appetite for different kinds of reading entertainment. Manga books—slim volumes bound in silk, with numerous drawings accompanied by explanatory text—became popular, especially those about glamorous actresses and actors.

Because manga account for such a large sector of the Japanese publishing market, there are manga tailored to every age and interest. Approximately one out of every three books published in Japan is a manga. They can be bought at any newsstand for $3 or $4. Sales during the year 2002 totaled nearly $5 billion, more than 32 percent of the total revenue for all publications in Japan. Often published weekly, many manga are the size of a small telephone book.

The Performing Arts

Japanese culture contains a wealth of performing arts, both traditional and modern, and embraces a wide variety of types. Among these are dance, instrumental and vocal music, theater, folk arts, and acrobatics. Some of these arts emerged as fine art forms, while others come from religious or popular culture. But no matter their origin, each of these performing arts provides fascinating glimpses into Japanese culture.

Gagaku and Bugaku

Classical *gagaku* music, which was introduced into Japan from China in the eighth century, is a combination of musical styles borrowed from

A *taiko* is a traditional Japanese drum, which is still popular among young people in Japan. There are several famous taiko groups that perform internationally.

Korea, Manchuria, Persia, India, and Indochina. A variety of wind, stringed, and percussion instruments are used in gagaku performances. When gagaku is accompanied by dance, it is called *bugaku*. This style can be performed by either a single dancer or one or more pairs of dancers. The dances themselves are very precise and often tell a story. They may be slow or lively, depending on whether they are ceremonial dances, military dances, or dances for children.

Noh Plays

The medieval dance form that originated in China before being brought to Japan is called Noh theater. Actors in Noh plays perform on a plain stage about 18 square feet (1.7 sq m) and on a narrow runway leading to the stage from the dressing room. Actors move across the stage very slowly, while reciting lines from ancient poetry. Today, many Japanese find Noh dramas difficult to understand because the chanting of words can be hard to decipher.

Actors are accompanied by drums, a high-pitched flute, and chanting by a chorus of six or eight men. All parts, including female roles, are played by men and boys. There are only two important character roles in a Noh drama: the *shite*, or principal character, and the *waki*, or subordinate character. Both the shite and the waki wear handsomely embroidered costumes. The shite also wears a painted wooden mask. The actor's emotions are expressed by slight movements of the mask on the face. Different masks are used to represent men, women, elderly persons, gods, and demons. Even without being able to understand what is being said, a Noh play is a spectacular experience filled with drama, beauty, and the poetry of motion.

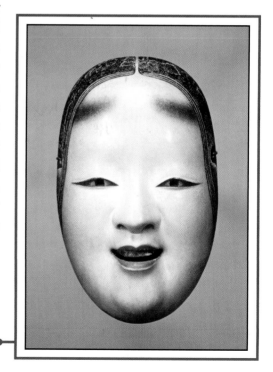

This is a Momoyama-period mask that was used in Noh theater. This mask dates back to the mid-sixteenth century. Noh is still very popular today. There are around 1,500 professional Noh actors currently working in Japan.

A Bunraku play is performed with puppets in a theater in Tokyo. Bunraku puppeteers train their entire lives to perform in this style of theater. It takes great skill and technique to control the puppets.

Bunraku

Bunraku, or puppet dramas, date from the late seventeenth century in Japan. In this form of theater, puppets tell a story to the accompaniment of a shamisen, a three-stringed, banjo-shaped instrument.

The puppets used in Bunraku are nearly half life-size. They are handled by a team of three adults. By manipulating the strings inside the puppet's head, one person controls the movable mouth, eyebrows, and eyelids, as well as the right arm and hand of the doll. Meanwhile, assistants animate the rest of the puppet. The puppeteers speak no lines, but are visible to the audience throughout the play. Sometimes, two of them are seated on a wheeled stool from which they are able to move around the third seated puppeteer.

Unlike Noh performances, Bunraku shows use elaborate scenery. Today, Bunraku performances are not as common as they used to be, but there is the National Theater for Bunraku in Tokyo, and sometimes special companies tour throughout the world. The art form is regarded as a "cultural property" by the Japanese government, which regularly telecasts performances on Japanese television.

This painting from 1890 depicts the famous Kabuki actor Danjuro Ichikawa IX performing the role of Benkei in the play *Kanjincho* (The Subscription List). Ichikawa was popular during the Meiji era.

Kabuki

Kabuki theater originated in Japan around the same time as Bunraku. The early origins of the theater began in Kyoto, where a woman performed a series of dances on stage. However, deciding that the performances were immoral, the Japanese government outlawed women appearing in Kabuki theater. Women's roles were taken over by men, a practice that still continues. Over time, changes were also made to the Noh stage for Kabuki. This included the addition of a curtain and a *hanamichi,* or catwalk through the audience. These changes allowed the actors to make dramatic entrances and exits. Even though Kabuki theater was influenced by the aristocratic Noh theater, Kabuki was mostly seen as popular entertainment for the masses.

Kabuki performers are highly skilled actors who have been trained since childhood in dance, vocals, and acrobatics. The actors who play female roles are known as *onnagata* or *oyama*. Performances are held on a revolving stage. They are quite spectacular and very colorful. Scenery and actors rise from or disappear into the stage floor on elevators. In some Kabuki plays, the actors wear striking white, red, and black makeup to create the effect of power and strength. Elaborate costumes—which are often changed onstage—may weigh as much as 50 pounds (about 23 kilograms). As actors strike dramatic poses, they are accompanied by the beating of wooden clappers on the stage.

Traditional Kabuki is very melodramatic and tells historical stories. These old stories and the characters in the plays are often very familiar to those in the audience, even though the language can be difficult to follow. During performances, some audience members call out the school or family name of the actor. These responses are always done in a timely fashion so as not to interrupt the performance. Kabuki remains one of the most unique and breathtaking theatrical performances that exists.

FAMOUS FOODS AND RECIPES OF JAPAN

9

Traditional Japanese cuisine consists of a diet based on rice and noodles. Japanese cooking also draws on the available seafood found in the waters surrounding the islands. No matter what the meal, the Japanese place great importance on the way food is served and presented. When attractively done, a meal is as much a visual experience as it is a culinary one for the diner.

Traditional Foods

Most Japanese eat three meals a day. Boiled white rice (*gohan*), the mainstay of the Japanese diet for centuries, is eaten at almost every meal. However, in recent years, rice consumption per capita has declined considerably in favor of such Western staples as pasta and bread.

Tofu, a soybean product, is also a staple in Japanese kitchens. Many Japanese like using tofu because it is so versatile; it can be served hot or cold, salted or sweet, as a solid food or as a drink. Noodles, which were introduced into Japanese cuisine by the Chinese, are also an important element of Japanese cuisine. There are many types of noodles available for cooking, including *soba*, or buckwheat, and *udon*, a plump, white wheat noodle.

At left, a merchant hangs fresh squid in a seafood market in Atsumicho in the Yamagata Prefecture. Squid is prepared in a variety of ways in Japanese cuisine. Above, factory workers at a distillery stir a big vat of sake. Sake, a rice wine, originated sometime during the third century. There are many different types of sake, which is a very popular drink in Japan.

This is a photo of a traditional Japanese table. Sushi and sashimi are prepared and served on decorative plates. Painted bowls and cups are used for tea, sauces, and side dishes. Sushi is vinegared rice (rice with vinegar) with raw seafood or vegetables on top. Sashimi is a plate of raw fish.

Mealtimes

A traditional breakfast in Japan consists of rice, which is usually supplemented by *misoshiru*, a bean-paste soup, and *tsukemono*, pickled vegetables. Lunch is usually a light meal, which may consist of tsukemono, salted fish, and *tsukudani*, seafood or vegetables cooked and preserved in soy sauce, in addition to rice or noodles. Because Japanese businesspeople tend to work later than North Americans, dinner is served late at night. In most homes, dinner includes vegetables and rice with fish, beef, pork, or chicken.

Seasonings are important in Japanese cooking. These include seaweed and *wasabi*, or horseradish. Fruits are important, too, such as oranges (mandarin or clementine), persimmons, Fuji or Mutsu apples, pears, cherries, strawberries, plums, and melons. Japanese cuisine includes a lot of vegetables, including seaweed, giant white radish, cabbage, leek, spinach, and ginger root.

This is a bowl of powdered green tea with rakugan. Traditionally, tea ceremonies were very spiritual. Now, green tea is also known for its health benefits.

Drinking tea is an important ceremony in Japan, dating back hundreds of years. Japanese teahouses, in which the tea ceremony is observed, are found throughout the country. The tea used during this kind of ceremony

Okonomiyaki
(Japanese-style Pancakes)

Ingredients

¼ of a small cabbage
1 egg

¾ c. soup stock (*dashi*) or water
1 c. all-purpose flour

For Toppings

Thinly sliced pork or beef
Squid
Shrimp or dried shrimp (*sakura-ebi*)
Okonomiyaki sauce (or *tonkatsu* sauce)

Mayonnaise
Katsuo-bushi (dried bonito flakes)
Aonori (green seaweed)
Beni-shoga (red ginger)

Preparation

Cut the cabbage into very thin slices.
Beat the egg in a bowl and add dashi soup stock or water to it.
Add flour to the bowl and mix well.
Combine sliced cabbage in the flour mixture.
Fry meat/squid/shrimp (your choice of toppings) in an electric cooking pan or a frying pan.
Pour the flour mixture over the toppings in the pan. (Makes a couple of pancakes.)
Cook a few minutes and flip pancakes, then cook for a few more minutes.
Put okonomiyaki sauce and mayonnaise on top of the pancakes.
Sprinkle katsuo-bushi flakes, aonori, and beni-shoga on top.

Daifuku
(Sweet Rice Cake with Red Beans)

Ingredients

1 c. sweet rice flour (*mochiko*)

½ c. sugar

1 c. boiling water

Sweet red bean paste
  (*anko*) shaped into walnut-
  sized balls

Potato starch (*katakuriko*)

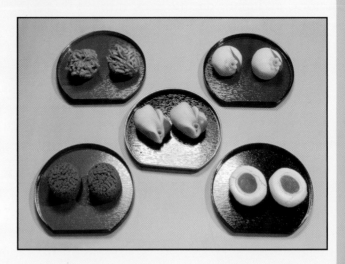

Preparation

Combine flour and sugar.

Add boiling water; mix well
  with wooden spoon.

Line prepared steamer with clean, damp dishcloth.

Place mixture into steamer. Steam for 25 minutes.

Remove from steamer onto board sprinkled with potato starch. Break off
  dough into golf-ball-sized pieces and flatten in palm of hand, leaving a
  shallow well in center.

Put sweet red bean paste ball in center of dough and bring edges of dough
  up and around the paste.

Pinch tightly to close.

Serve.

Sweet red bean paste can be found in Asian markets, as can sweet rice flour
and potato starch.

must be a powdered green tea that is grown in the Kyoto region. The host carries the tea and the utensils into the tearoom, where they are placed in designated places. While the water is heated over a charcoal fire, the host and guest sit on the *tatami* (straw matting) floor. The host then pours the water over the tea powder and whips it with a whisk. In addition, special sweet cakes such as Abekawa-mochi are served with the tea.

Eating Out

Many Japanese enjoy eating out, and they have a great variety of restaurants to choose from. For instance, *yakitori* restaurants feature chicken and vegetables served in chunks that are grilled over a charcoal fire on thin skewers. At *sukiyaki* restaurants, diners have their food cooked right at the table. The food is then dipped in assorted sauces.

The Japanese are no strangers to the idea of fast food. However, for many years, eating on the go usually meant going to a nearby noodle or sushi shop. Recently, many Japanese, especially children and teens in large cities, enjoy going to Western fast-food places such as McDonald's.

At a fast-food noodle shop, a customer puts coins in a machine in exchange for a ticket. Then the ticket is given to the chef, who prepares the soup.

Miso Soup

Ingredients

4 c. dashi soup stock
½ package tofu
3 tbsp. miso paste
¼ c. chopped green onion

Preparation

Put the soup stock in a pan and bring to a boil.
Cut tofu into small cubes and add them to the soup.
Scoop out some soup stock from the pan and dissolve miso paste in it.
Return the soup-miso mixture to the pan.
Take the pan off the heat and add chopped green onion.

DAILY LIFE AND CUSTOMS IN JAPAN

10

At a time when growing urbanization and technology make it harder for people to talk to each other, the Japanese continue to practice the teachings of Confucianism. At the same time, however, the Japanese walk between two worlds: the old and the new. This approach demonstrates the Japanese respect for tradition as well as a willingness to adopt new ideas and practices.

The Importance of the Group

There is an old Japanese saying that states, "The nail that sticks up gets hammered down." This proverb sums up an important characteristic of Japanese people: their intense loyalty to groups and their dislike of individualism. Japanese life has always focused on family and groups. Even today, family ties remain strong and it is not uncommon for several generations to live under one roof. Next to one's family, the most important group in Japan is the company or business that one works for. In addition to family and work groups, most Japanese also participate in other organized group activities, such as clubs devoted to a hobby. The Japanese are also enthusiastic tourists, and trips are often taken as a group.

At left, a sumo match draws large crowds to the Kokugikan stadium in Tokyo. Fans of sumo wrestling will spend up to ten hours at the stadium before the match to make sure they get a good seat. Because sumo is such a popular sport, tickets usually sell out within a few hours of going on sale. Above is a scene from director Hayao Miyazaki's *Spirited Away*. This film was the highest-grossing domestic film in Japan's history.

The Importance of Traditional Values

Japanese people are very conscious of their behavior and manners. The Japanese commonly show their respect by bowing. The deeper the bow, the higher the social position or amount of respect of the person is shown.

In Japan, the notion of harmony is also very important and is considered to be the key to maintaining good relations within a group. Disgracing oneself, or "losing face," is something of great shame in Japanese society. Instances such as losing a job or failing an exam, as well as cheating or engaging in dishonest behavior, are not only a source of embarrassment for the individual, but can also cast shame upon a person's family and name.

Family Life

The Japanese live a life filled with tradition and ritual from the time they are born until they die. When a baby is about three days old, it is named in a small ceremony in which friends and relatives bring gifts. At the age of about one month, the child is taken to the nearest Shinto shrine, where the priest records the child's name and birthday. This means the child is now formally recognized as a member of the community.

When a couple decides to marry, a ceremonial exchange of engagement gifts, or *yuino*, takes place. The marriage ceremony is usually Shinto. The bride, who wears a

white kimono (a loose-fitting garment with wide sleeves), and the groom, who is also clothed in traditional dress, take three sips of sake from three cups. This ceremony is usually followed by feasting and dancing.

When a person dies, he or she is often buried according to Buddhist rites. Virtually all Japanese are cremated. The urn containing the deceased's ashes is then placed on an altar at the family's house and kept there for forty-nine days, after which the urn is usually buried in a Buddhist cemetery.

A bride is dressed for her wedding pictures at the Meiji-jingu shrine in Tokyo. The Meiji-jingu shrine is a popular place for Japanese couples to get married or have their pictures taken. It is considered one of the most beautiful Shinto shrines in Tokyo.

Japanese Homes

Traditional Japanese homes are built from very light materials and are designed to let in as much air and sunlight as possible. Walls are often made of wood and paper panels that slide open or can be entirely removed. Though pleasant in the summer, they lack central heating and are cold in the winter. Traditionally, Japanese sleep on thick, heavy comforters called futons that they stretch out on the floor. During the day, the bedding is easily folded up and stored in a closet. The floors of traditional Japanese

In the Shimane Prefecture, the Iwao family sits down to dinner after a hard day of work making washi paper. Idani, their son, will likely take over his father's washi business after he retires.

rooms are covered with thick mats of rush straw called tatami. A typical home in a Japanese city is quite small, averaging less than 200 square feet (19 sq m) in Tokyo.

Style

Modern Japanese dress incorporates Eastern and Western styles for men and women. The traditional kimono is now worn principally on certain special occasions such as weddings, New Year's Day, and funerals. *Geta*, or raised wooden clogs, and *zori*, rubber or straw sandals, are still worn with kimonos. Socks called *tabi* are worn with geta and zori.

Beginning in the late 1970s and early 1980s, Japanese fashion design played a major role in redefining contemporary international fashion. These designs incorporated both traditional Japanese costume and craft traditions with an eye to the modern lifestyle of the Japanese.

An 1895 drawing illustrates Buddhist monks carrying prayer beads beside women in traditional Japanese dress. The women place long, decorative pins in their hair and carry fans.

Some Japanese baseball stars continue their careers in America. In this photograph, Ichiro Suzuki bats for the Seattle Mariners in a game against the New York Mets. Ichiro was the first Japanese-born position player in American major league baseball. Before moving to Seattle, he played for nine years in Japan's Pacific League.

Sports

Practically every Western form of athletics is enjoyed in Japan. The most popular Western sport is baseball, which the Japanese call *yakyu*. Professional baseball teams are sponsored by business firms and have English names such as the Giants, Dragons, and Bay Stars. The Japanese are also avid golfers. During the winter, many Japanese head to mountain resorts to ski.

The Japanese also enjoy watching traditional sporting events. Sumo wrestling is one of the country's most popular sports. Several professional sumo tournaments are held each year in the big cities.

Having Fun

The Japanese enjoy a wide range of leisure activities and pursuits. Almost every Japanese household has at least one television set. Japanese networks present general-interest programs, such as news, drama, comedy, and quiz shows. North

A movie still from the 1954 classic film *Godzilla*. Godzilla is a monster that was created as a result of American nuclear experimentation.

American movies and TV shows are very popular in Japan, with Japanese voices dubbed in.

The Japanese are exceptionally avid readers. Average daily newspaper circulation amounts to about one copy for every two people. This ratio is among the highest in the world and almost twice that of the United States.

While many Japanese movies have become internationally famous for their artistic and technical quality, other films, particularly monster movies, are also very popular. During the 1950s and 1960s, several Japanese prehistoric-type monsters found their way to the movie screens. The most popular include Godzilla, the giant insect Mothra, Rodan, Gamera, and Gorgo.

One of the most famous of Japanese film directors is Akira Kurosawa. He is considered by many to be one of the most influential filmmakers of the late twentieth century. In 1951,

This is a movie still from the 1954 classic *Seven Samurai*, by Akira Kurosawa. On the far left is renowned actor Toshiro Mifune.

Two young boys practice kendo during their martial arts class at Osaka Castle. Kendo was developed during the sixteenth century. It focuses on the techniques and artistry of sword fighting.

Kurosawa single-handedly introduced the West to Japanese cinema with his movies depicting stories of samurai and life in old Japan.

The Martial Arts

In Japan, many people practice martial arts, a system of self-defense. These forms originated with the samurai, who mastered at least one or two of them for use in battle. Today, many people practice them as competitive sports and for physical and mental fitness.

Among the more popular martial art forms that are practiced is judo. In competitions, the first person to lift his opponent over his shoulders, to pin him down until he gives up, or to pin him for at least thirty seconds is considered the victor. Colored belts are worn to indicate degrees of mastery in judo.

Kyudo, or archery, was used in early Japan for fishing and hunting. After the introduction of firearms in the sixteenth century, however, kyudo declined as an effective technique of combat and became a sport. Kyudo archers use a 7-foot (2 m) bow made of wood glued to bamboo. Arrows consist of a bamboo shaft, three feathers, and an arrowhead.

EDUCATION AND WORK IN JAPAN

E ducation, which is taken very seriously in Japan, is considered to be one of the most important reasons for the nation's economic success. Helping to prepare students to meet the challenges of new technology and work within the international world is one reason why Japan has enjoyed this success. To help maintain high standards, the Ministry of Education regularly compares Japan's level of educational achievement with those of other nations. The office is not satisfied unless Japan ranks at or near the top, and it constantly pressures its schools to raise

their standards. As a result, Japanese schools have earned international praise for achieving near 100 percent literacy year after year. This is a rare occurrence for any nation. In the year 2000, Japan ranked highest in most subjects in a comparison study of fifteen-year-olds from thirty-one countries around the world. Japan placed first in math and second in science, after South Korea.

Early Education

The Japanese public school system is organized into three levels: national, prefecture or state, and local. The modern school system was introduced in 1868. By 1872, elementary and secondary schools had been established throughout the country. Free

At left, a woman makes somen (thin noodles) in Hyogo, Japan. Above, schoolchildren visit a memorial to the victims of the 1945 Hiroshima atomic bombing. In Japan, schoolchildren are often taken on a weeklong visit to historic places before graduation.

These children are learning to play recorders and keyboards in elementary school. Music is an important part of education in Japan. Until the end of high school, all Japanese students are required to study music.

compulsory education began in 1900. Beginning at age six, all children in Japan must attend six-year elementary schools and three-year junior high schools. This means that all children attend school from kindergarten through the ninth grade. About 94 percent of Japanese schoolchildren go on to attend senior high schools.

Education in Japan is known for being very demanding, even more than it is in the North America. The school year begins on April 1 and is divided into three terms: April to July, September to December, and January to March. The school year lasts thirty-five weeks, with a short summer vacation of one month. Discipline in the schools is strict, and daily homework is assigned from the first grade on. Nine subjects are studied: Japanese language, mathematics, social studies, science, music, arts, morals training, and special activities. Physical education is also taught, especially judo, kendo, and sumo. About half of all students receive outside tutoring or attend afterschool academies for further instruction.

Beginning in 2002, however, the Japanese school day underwent a dramatic change. Despite protests by parents and some students, Japan's 2,110 public elementary

This photo of kindergarten children illustrates a common occurence throughout Japan—waiting in line. When waiting in Japan, most people will line up in an orderly fashion.

and secondary schools cut back the school week to Monday through Friday only, doing away with Saturday classes. Under the new plan, 100 hours are cut from the school year, and the workload for the students was reduced by as much as 30 percent. But in place of the extra free day, Japanese students are required to participate in at least three hours of extracurricular activities such as sports.

"Examination Hell"

Students who wish to continue their education after junior high school must pass difficult entrance exams for senior high school and university. The pressure to pass these exams, which are given in February and March each year, is so great that the Japanese call it *juhen jigoku* or "examination hell." These exams place students under enormous pressure. Some begin preparing for the exam as early as the first grade. Critics of the examinations blame the rising suicide rate among Japanese youths, which is now the world's highest, on the tests and their outcome.

Students at Juku (cram school) prepare for exams by listening intently as a professor demonstrates a scientific experiment. The students range in age from eight to eighteen. There are cram schools for every level of schooling.

Despite the criticism of this system, during the examination season, families with sons or daughters taking the exams are caught up in the excitement. Experts appear on TV talk shows to give advice to parents. Newspapers and magazines report on the numbers of high schools with students advancing to universities. Exam results are posted on school bulletin boards. Anxious parents and their children begin to gather around the schools twenty-four hours in advance. When the results are put up, some people fear to look. If a student has succeeded, the parents will be all smiles. If not, they will be terribly gloomy. Those students who do not pass are known as *ronin*, named after wandering samurai who had no masters. Students who fail often enroll in special "cram" schools, known as *yobiko*. They will study more and try again the next year.

Apart from entrance exams, competition in Japanese schools is limited. Grades are not given much importance, and differences in ability are played down. Hardly anyone flunks out. Students who get into the top universities often let their studies slide for a while. This is perhaps in reaction to the punishing years of secondary education. In addition to their classes, students may spend time doing sports, hobbies, or political activities. Eventually, though, most settle down and study for the next round of exams in preparation for entering the business world or government service.

Education and Careers

About 48 percent of all Japanese high school graduates continue to study at universities. In the United States, the rate is about 50 percent. Overall, the percentage of Japanese high school students going on to receive some type of further education, whether at a university, trade school, junior college, or correspondence school, is much higher—72 percent. The Japanese have an even more compelling reason for pursuing education. In no other society does a successful career in business or government depend so much on a person's education. The best companies and the most important government ministries recruit the graduates of the top-ranking universities and virtually assure them of lifetime jobs.

The system of higher education in Japan, as elsewhere, includes universities, colleges, junior colleges, and schools for vocational and technical training. The modern educational system was established after the Meiji Restoration of 1868 and was consciously modeled on higher education in Europe and the United States. In Japan, the most prestigious schools are the national, or public, universities. Entrance to the national universities is based on merit, rather than one's social class or the ability to pay.

Tokyo University is Japan's most prestigious university. The university is best known for its law school and its literature department.

As a result, these universities draw the best students from all walks of life. The schools are ranked, and examinations to get into the better schools are extremely competitive. Those students who fail the examinations study hard to take them again rather than settle for a less desirable school. The courses of study are considered mild compared to the effort it takes to pass the entrance examination. Once accepted, students normally spend their whole college career in one school, even in one department of the school.

Specialization in scientific and technological studies is encouraged. Employment after graduation is rarely a problem. Those who graduate from other universities, or vocational or trade schools, usually settle for lesser jobs, but they, too, can count on security and white-collar status. As a result, almost every student who wants a future seeks to enter a university, where there is only room for two out of every five applicants.

Work Life in Japan

The Japanese way of doing business fosters a spirit of cooperation rather than competition. At the white-collar level, after graduation junior executives are recruited from the top-ranking universities. Often, their scores on company examinations are less important than the fact that they attended the same school as their employers. For this reason, employers believe that a new employee will not only be loyal, but will contribute to the overall harmony of the workplace.

On a warm spring day in Tokyo, people picnic beneath beautiful cherry blossoms.

On a typical workday in smaller businesses and factories, the employees begin the day with some physical exercise, often followed by songs or cheers to boost morale. Employees often work in small groups, with each group assigned a specific task or problem to solve. Regardless of status in the company, all workers are encouraged to make suggestions. Failures or mistakes are not dwelled upon. Instead, they are seen as something you can learn from.

On average, Japanese workers work six weeks longer than North Americans. While they enjoy time off for national holidays, rarely do they take extended vacations. Average workdays for white-collar workers can last as long as eighteen hours. Work-related stress can lead to *karoshi*, or death by overwork. Today, many companies do not ask as much of their workers. They have cut back on worker hours and allow more time for hobbies or family. In periods when the economy is slumping, many companies introduced five-day weeks, "casual Fridays," and reduced overtime. In recent years, the government has also added more public holidays.

The "Salaryman"

A businessman employed by a company is known in Japan as a salaryman. This means that the worker is a successful white-collar employee who can count on

After a long, hard day of work, salarymen sleep or read on the subway ride home in Tokyo. Some salarymen work up to sixteen hours a day. That's twice the average workday in the United States and Canada.

a regular paycheck regardless of how the economy or business is doing. Job security encourages an employee's loyalty. However, it also has a downside in that companies can't fire lazy or unproductive workers, though the practice is somewhat changing.

The company provides a typical salaryman with sickness and accident benefits and a retirement pension. The salaryman must be committed to his company; not only does he attend all company functions, but at least once a year, he travels to the countryside with other employees. These trips are used to work out any problems that may exist between workers and to ensure that the workplace remains a harmonious environment.

Blue-collar Workers

Blue-collar workers, or workers who are skilled tradesmen, enjoy many of the same benefits as salarymen. Instead of separate unions that represent a particular craft or trade, each large company has a union that represents all workers. This union is often affiliated with a nationwide labor federation. Because the company guarantees workers job security, union members tend to identify with the company's interests rather than those of the labor unions. Employees may bargain for higher wages and better working conditions, but as a rule, they do not strike against the company. This treatment of union workers in Japan is very successful; the number of workdays lost in strikes is less than a third of that in the United States and Great Britain.

Another difference is that union members do not oppose new technology. They know that if their old skills are no longer needed, the company will train them in new skills. A company that wants good relations between management and workers will rarely lay off workers. As a result, in recent decades the rate of unemployment in Japan has usually been below 5.5 percent.

A woman picks tea leaves in the hot sun in Wakayama. Tea harvesters are usually paid for each pound of tea that they pick instead of receiving a flat daily wage.

JAPAN
AT A GLANCE

HISTORY

The history of Japan dates back to at least 100,000 years ago. During the Jomon period (10,500 BC to 300 BC), the inhabitants of Japan were primarily hunter-gatherers and fishermen. The Yayoi period (300 BC to AD 300) saw the introduction of the rice culture into Japan. Over time, social classes began emerging, while iron was introduced from Korea. Historical records show that Japan was unified as a nation by the late fourth or early fifth century AD, when the Yamato dynasty claimed power. During the Yamato period, Japan borrowed heavily from Chinese influences, including Buddhism and the Chinese system of writing. During the Heian period of the ninth to twelfth centuries, the Fujiwara clan came to power, at which time a new class—the samurai warrior—emerged. By the end of the twelfth century, Japan was ruled by a shogun or chief military commander; the government was called a shogunate.

During the period of the shogunate, Japan established trade contacts with other countries such as Spain, England, and Holland. The arrival of the Portuguese during the sixteenth century not only introduced trade, but Christianity as well. However, fearing that Japan could be conquered by a foreign nation, a new shogunate of the period forbade any further trade with foreign powers. Accordingly, Japan was once more isolated from the world. By the mid-nineteenth century, however, the shogunate was unable to keep European and American traders away.

In 1868, a new government was established under the young emperor Mutsuhito, who took the name of Meiji, meaning "enlightened government." The Meiji period marked the beginning of Japan's modern era and would last until 1912. Soon, Japan embarked on a program of expansion and successfully fought two wars: one with China from 1894 to 1895 and one with Russia from 1904 to 1905. In both instances, Japan won territory.

During the 1930s and 1940s, the Japanese government seized territory in China and French Indochina (now Vietnam.) In December 1941, Japanese planes

112

attacked the United States forces at Pearl Harbor, Hawaii, after which the United States declared war on Japan. In August 1945, the United States dropped atomic bombs on the Japanese cities of Hiroshima and Nagasaki. As a result, the Japanese surrendered.

Under the terms of surrender, Japan was forced to give up all the territory it had acquired since 1895. In addition, United States forces occupied the country until 1952. In 1947, a new constitution gave a lot of power to the elected legislature and took power away from the emperor.

In time, Japan rebuilt its ruined economy, using new technology in every major industry. By the 1990s, Japan had one of the world's largest economies and had emerged as one of the world's leading economic, technological, and industrial nations.

This plaque marks where the Nakajima District in Hiroshima used to be before it was bombed on August 6, 1945. It is now the site of the Peace Memorial Park.

ECONOMY

Initially, the Japanese economy was largely agricultural and there was little in the way of trade relations with other countries. However, by the time of the Meiji Restoration in 1868, while Japan was still predominantly an agricultural economy, it had also built up some commerce. These industries were limited to the production of foodstuffs, textiles, and household items. Goods such as soy, sake, candles, cotton cloth, and silk textiles were produced in workshops organized by family monopolies or craft guilds. These guilds specialized in the production of a particular good such as cloth or candles. In time, the government established and operated shipyards, arsenals, machine shops, foundries such as iron and steel mills, and cotton mills. These industries were later sold to private interests.

During the 1920s and 1930s, heavy industries in Japan greatly expanded, due to Japan's growing need to broaden its empire. With its defeat in World War II, Japan's economy collapsed. But just a decade later, the nation reemerged as a major industrial power. By the 1970s, it had become the most industrialized country in Asia and the second greatest economic power in the world, after the United States.

As manufacturing and industry were on the rise, the agricultural economy was declining. By 2003, agricultural industry was less than 5 percent of total production in Japan and accounted for less than 2 percent of the GNP (gross national product). Part of the problem is that Japanese farmland is overworked and exhausted. Farm products that are grown and sold include rice, some vegetables, and industrial crops used for manufacturing, such as mulberry trees for silk. Livestock is also raised. Commercial fishing is also very important to the Japanese economy, and the annual catch by Japanese fishers is among the largest in the world.

Japanese industry depends heavily on raw materials from other countries. Imports include machinery and equipment, fuels, foodstuffs, chemicals, and textiles. Manufactured goods make up the vast majority of the nation's exports—machinery, motor vehicles, ships, and steel are among the items sent abroad. By the 1980s, Japan was a leading exporter of high-tech goods, including electrical and electronic appliances. During the late twentieth century, Japan shifted some of its industries—such as automobile manufacturing—overseas. They also invested in real estate abroad, especially in the United States, western Canada, and the Pacific Rim countries, such as Australia and New Zealand. Japan has also become a global leader in financial services, with some of the world's largest banks.

GOVERNMENT AND POLITICS

The current government of Japan is based on the constitution of 1947. This was drafted by the American military authorities and approved by the Japanese diet, known as the Kokkai, a parliamentary body that holds sole legislative power in Japan. The diet is composed of the House of Representatives, or the Shugi-in—a body of 480 members elected for terms of four years, with 300 representatives elected from single-seat constituencies and the rest proportionally according to

Car manufacturing is a very important industry in Japan. Cars are a major Japanese export.

the size of their prefecture, or legislative district. The other governing body is the house of councilors, or Sangi-in, composed of 247 members elected for terms of six years. The executive body of Japan consists of an eighteen-member cabinet appointed and headed by the prime minister, who is elected by the Kokkai. The prime minister usually represents the leader of the majority party in the Kokkai. A Supreme Court heads the judicial system in Japan. During the twentieth century, Japan has had two emperors: Hirohito, who ruled from 1926 until his death in 1989, and his son, Akihito, who succeeded him.

On the local and regional levels, Japan is divided into forty-seven prefectures that are similar to states or provinces. Each prefecture has a popularly elected governor and a unicameral, or one-house legislature. Cities, towns, and villages elect their own mayors and assemblies. Political parties in Japan are numerous, and almost 10,000 parties are active on the local and regional level. Political parties tend to be quite small in number and lack the broad, mass memberships as seen in North America or Great Britain. Members of Japanese political parties also tend to be professional or career politicians.

TIMELINE

10,500 BC
Jomon society.

10,000 BC
Stone Age in Aichi and Tochigi.

300 BC
Yayoi period begins.

AD 300s
Yamato period begins.

369
Japanese colony of Mimana established in Korea.

538
Buddhism introduced into Japan.

607
First Buddhist temples built in Nara.

710
Nara becomes the capital.

794
Kyoto becomes the capital. The Heian period begins.

858
The Fujiwara clan takes power.

1000
Shikibu Murasaki writes *The Tale of Genji*.

1614
Christianity banned.

1635
Interaction with foreigners banned except at the port of Nagasaki.

1641
All but Chinese and Dutch are banned from Japan.

1707
Last eruption of Mount Fuji.

1853
Commodore Matthew Perry steams into Edo (Tokyo) Bay and demands trade.

1868
Restoration of imperial rule (Meiji Restoration). Tokyo becomes capital.

1887
Torakusu Yamaha starts reed organ manufacturer, which becomes the modern diversified Yamaha Corporation.

1894–1895
First Chinese-Japanese War.

1946
Masaru Ibuka and Akio Morita found Sony Corporation.

1947
New constitution of Japan ratified.

1952
American occupation of Japan ends.

1964
Olympic Games held in Tokyo. Shinkansen (bullet train) starts operating.

1972
Winter Olympics held in Sapporo. Okinawa reverts to Japan from the United States.

1985
Yen rises in world market.

1988
Emperor Hirohito dies. Akihito ascends to the throne the following year.

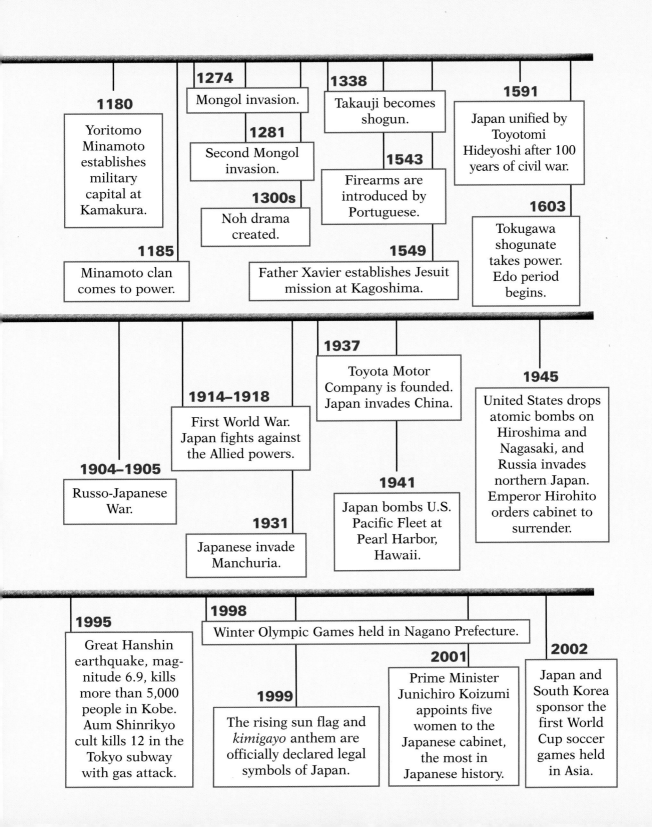

1180
Yoritomo Minamoto establishes military capital at Kamakura.

1274
Mongol invasion.

1281
Second Mongol invasion.

1300s
Noh drama created.

1185
Minamoto clan comes to power.

1338
Takauji becomes shogun.

1543
Firearms are introduced by Portuguese.

1549
Father Xavier establishes Jesuit mission at Kagoshima.

1591
Japan unified by Toyotomi Hideyoshi after 100 years of civil war.

1603
Tokugawa shogunate takes power. Edo period begins.

1904–1905
Russo-Japanese War.

1914–1918
First World War. Japan fights against the Allied powers.

1931
Japanese invade Manchuria.

1937
Toyota Motor Company is founded. Japan invades China.

1941
Japan bombs U.S. Pacific Fleet at Pearl Harbor, Hawaii.

1945
United States drops atomic bombs on Hiroshima and Nagasaki, and Russia invades northern Japan. Emperor Hirohito orders cabinet to surrender.

1995
Great Hanshin earthquake, magnitude 6.9, kills more than 5,000 people in Kobe. Aum Shinrikyo cult kills 12 in the Tokyo subway with gas attack.

1998
Winter Olympic Games held in Nagano Prefecture.

1999
The rising sun flag and *kimigayo* anthem are officially declared legal symbols of Japan.

2001
Prime Minister Junichiro Koizumi appoints five women to the Japanese cabinet, the most in Japanese history.

2002
Japan and South Korea sponsor the first World Cup soccer games held in Asia.

JAPAN

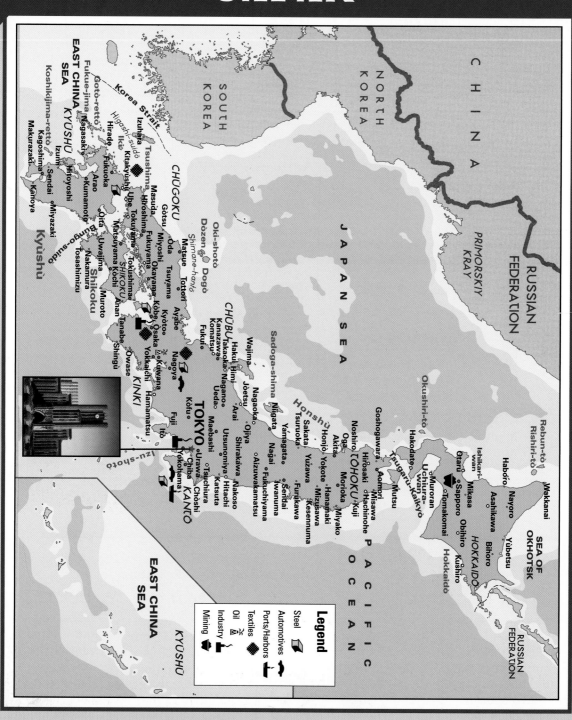

RUSSIAN FEDERATION

CHINA

NORTH KOREA

SOUTH KOREA

Korea Strait

EAST CHINA SEA

KYŪSHŪ

Koshikijima-rettō
Makurazaki
Kanoya
Kagoshima
Izumi
Sendai
Hitoyoshi
Arao
Kumamoto
Nagasaki
Fukue-jima
Fukue
Gotō-rettō
Hirado
Ikie
Fukuoka
Higashi-suidō
Izuhara
Tsushima
Kitakyūshū
Ube
Tokuyama
Hiroshima
Fukuyama
Okayama
Kōbe
Ōsaka
Kyoto
Kuwana
Nagoya
Yokkaichi

Kyūshū

Bungo-suidō
Ōita
Uwajima
Nakamura
Tosashimizu
Shingu
Ōwase
Tanabe
Hamamatsu
KINKI
Fuji
Kōfu
Itō
Kōchi
Muroto
Anan
Tokushima
Matsuyama
SHIKOKU

Shikoku

Masuda
Gōtsu
Miyoshi
Ōda
Tsuyama
Matsue
Tottori
Ayabe
Komatsu
Kanazawa
Takaoka
Nagano
Ueda
Maebashi
Katsuta

CHŪGOKU

Oki-shotō
Dōzen
Dōgō
Shimane-hantō

Sadoga-shima

CHŪBU
Hakui
Himi
Wajima
Jōetsu
Nagaoka
Niigata
Ojiya
Arai
Shirakawa
Aizuwakamatsu
Sendai
Fukuchiyama
Nagai
Yamagata
Tsuruoka
Yuzawa
Sakata
Honjō
Akita
Oga
Noshiro

Utsunomiya
Hitachi
Tsuchiura
Urawa
Chiba
Yokohama
Chōshi
TOKYO
KANTŌ

Izu-shotō

HONSHŪ Honshū

JAPAN SEA

Yokote
Hanamaki
Mizusawa
Morioka
Miyako
Kuji
TOHOKU TŌHOKU
Hachinohe
Hirosaki
Misawa
Aomori
Mutsu
Goshogawara

Kesennuma
Iwanuma

PRIMORSKIY KRAY

Okushiri-tō

Tsugaru-Kaikyō
Hakodate
Uchiura-wan
Muroran
Tomakomai
Sapporo
Otaru
Ishikari-wan
Mikasa
Asahikawa
Bihoro
Kushiro
Obihiro
HOKKAIDŌ

Hokkaidō

Yūbetsu
Haboro
Nayoro

Rebun-tō
Rishiri-tō
Wakkanai

SEA OF OKHOTSK

RUSSIAN FEDERATION

PACIFIC OCEAN

EAST CHINA SEA

KYŪSHŪ

Legend

Steel

Automotives

Ports/Harbors

Textiles

Oil

Industry

Mining

ECONOMIC FACT SHEET

GDP in US$: $3.55 trillion

GDP Sectors: Services 68%, Industry 31%, Agriculture 1%

Land Use: Arable Land 12.13%, Permanent Crops 1.01%, Other 86.86%

Currency: Yen

Workforce: Services 70%, Industry 25%, Agriculture 5%

Major Agricultural Products: Rice, sugar beets, vegetables, fruit, pork, poultry, dairy products, eggs, fish

Major Exports: Motor vehicles, semiconductors, office machinery, chemicals

Major Imports: Machinery and equipment, fuels, foodstuffs, chemicals, textiles

Significant Trading Partners:

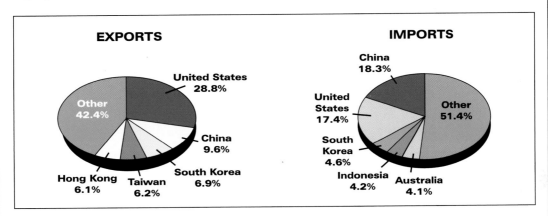

EXPORTS

- United States 28.8%
- China 9.6%
- South Korea 6.9%
- Taiwan 6.2%
- Hong Kong 6.1%
- Other 42.4%

IMPORTS

- China 18.3%
- United States 17.4%
- South Korea 4.6%
- Indonesia 4.2%
- Australia 4.1%
- Other 51.4%

Rate of Unemployment: 5.4%

Highways: Total 721,967 miles (1,161,894 km)

Railroads: Total 14,396 miles (23,168 km)

Waterways: Total 1,099 miles (1,770 km)

Airports: 172 (paved 141, unpaved 31), heliports 15

POLITICAL FACT SHEET

Official Country Name: Japan
Capital: Tokyo
System of Government:
Constitutional monarchy with
a parliamentary government
Federal Structure: Emperor,
prime minister, cabinet,
parliament known as the Diet,
made up of the House of
Councillors known as the
Sangi-in and the House of
Representatives, known as the
Shugi-in

Government Structure: Bicameral parliament composed of the Sangi-in and
the Shugi-in. Sangi-in has 247 seats, Shugi-in has 480 seats
National Anthem: *Kimigayo.* Lyrics from ancient poem "Kokinshu," music by
Hayashi Hiromori, circa 1880, adopted 1893

May the Emperor's reign,
Continue for a thousand, nay,
Eight thousand generations;
and for the eternity that it takes
For small pebbles to grow into a great rock
and become covered with moss.

Administrative Divisions: 47 prefectures: Aichi, Akita, Aomori, Chiba,
Ehime, Fukui, Fukuoka, Fukushima, Gifu, Gumma, Hiroshima, Hokkaido,
Hyogo, Ibaraki, Ishikawa, Iwate, Kagawa, Kagoshima, Kanagawa, Kochi,
Kumamoto, Kyoto, Mie, Miyagi, Miyazaki, Nagano, Nagasaki, Nara, Niigata,
Oita, Okayama, Okinawa, Osaka, Saga, Saitama, Shiga, Shimane, Shizuoka,
Tochigi, Tokushima, Tokyo, Tottori, Toyama, Wakayama, Yamagata,
Yamaguchi, Yamanashi
Independence: 660 BC
Constitution: May 3, 1947
Legal System: Based on European civil law system with English-American
influence, judicial review of legislative acts in the Supreme Court
Suffrage: 20 years of age, universal
Number of Registered Voters: In 2003, 100,492,328 out of a population of
126,919,288

CULTURAL FACT SHEET

Official Language: Japanese
Major Religions: Shinto and Buddhist 84%, other 16%, Christian .07%
Ethnic Groups: Japanese 99%, others 1% (includes Korean, Chinese, Brazilian, Filipino, and others)
Life Expectancy: Female 84 years, male 78 years
Time: Standard time is Greenwich Mean Time +9
Literacy Rate: 99%
National Flower: Cherry blossom
National Bird: Pheasant
National Butterfly: Giant purple butterfly
Cultural Leaders: Note to reader: it is customary in Japanese to name the surname first. However, we list the first names first.

> **Fashion Designers:** Issey Miyake, Yoji Yomamoto, Rei Kawakubo, Hanae Mori
>
> **Literature:** Osamu Dazai, Inoue Yasushi, Yasunari Kawabata, Yukio Mishima, Soseki Natsume, Naoya Shiga, Junichiro Tanizaki, Haruki Murakami
>
> **Entertainment:** Akira Kurosawa (director), Yoji Yamada (director), Oda Yuji (actor), Rie Miyazawa (actress), Nanako Matsushima (actress), Motoya Izumi (Noh actor), Masatoshi Nagase (actor), Masaharu Fukuyama (radio DJ), Hikaru Utada (musician/singer), Monta Mino (television host)
>
> **Sports:** Midori Ito (ice skater), Isao Aoki (golfer), Kazuhiro Sasaki (baseball player), Naoko Takahashi (runner), Asashoryu (sumo wrestler), Hideki Matsui (baseball player), Ichiro Suzuki (baseball player)

National Holidays and Festivals

Many Japanese holidays fall according to religious or nonstandard calendars, so the dates will vary from year to year.

January 1: Shogatsu (New Year's)
Second Monday of January: Seiji No Hi (Coming of Age Day)
February 4: Setsubun (beginning of Spring)
March 3: Hina-matsuri (Doll's Festival for Girls)
March 21: Shunbun No Hi (Spring Equinox Day). Graves are visited.
May 5: Kodomo No Hi (Children's Festival, formerly known as Boy's Festival Day)
August 13–16: Bon (The Feast of the Dead)

Third Monday of September: Keiro No Hi (Respect for the Aged Day) Respect for the elderly and longevity is celebrated on this national holiday.
Second Monday of October: Taiiku No Hi (Health and Sports Day) On this day in 1964, the Olympic Games in Tokyo opened.
November 15: Shichi-go-san (7-5-3 Day for Children)
December 31: Oomisoka (New Year's Eve)

GLOSSARY

animism (AN-ah-miz-em) The belief that all natural objects possess a soul.

arable (AYR-uh-bul) Fit for cultivation.

Bolshevik Revolution (BOL-shih-vek reh-vo-LOO-shun) Russian revolution that overthrew the czar and seized control of the government in 1917. The Bolsheviks were members of the Russian Social Democrat Party.

Buddhism (BOO-dism) Religion that teaches that selfishness is the cause of all sorrow; by renouncing worldly pleasures and goods, one can gain perfection and happiness.

bushido (boo-SHI-doh) The samurai "way of the warrior," which stresses self-discipline and loyalty.

chivalry (SHIV-all-ree) The set of qualities of the ideal knight, including honor, bravery, courtesy, and gallant behavior toward women.

Confucianism (con-FEW-shun-ism) A set of principles based on the teachings of Confucius that emphasize social harmony and justice.

daimyo (DAH-me-yo) Feudal lord of medieval Japan.

dashi (DA-she) One of many simple soup stocks used in Japanese cooking.

deity (DAY-uh-tee) God or goddess.

embodiment (em-BAH-dee-ment) The personification of someone or something.

feudalism (FEW-dahl-ism) A political and social system in which a landowner grants use of the land to a peasant in exchange for various other duties.

futon (FOO-tahn) Thick cotton mattress used as bedding in Japan.

GNP (gross national product) The value of all goods and services produced within a nation in a given year.

haiku (HI-koo) Three-line poem with 5, 7, and 5 syllables per line.

hibachi (he-BAH-chee) Metal or ceramic container used for heating Japanese homes.

homogenous (ho-MAH-jen-us) Of the same or similar kind.

hunter-gatherers (HUN-ter GATH-ers) A nomadic group that survives by hunting, fishing, and gathering fruits and nuts.

kana (KAHN-ah) Japanese phonetic script.

kanji (KAHN-jee) Chinese characters used for writing by the Japanese.

katsuobushi flakes (kat-soh-BOO-shee FLAYKS) Dried flakes made from smoked blocks of bonito fish, which is used as a topping for Japanese dishes.

kimono (kih-MO-no) Traditional Japanese garment worn by men and women; a robe with wide sleeves and a broad sash.

lacquer (LAK-er) A type of varnish made from the sap of the lacquer tree.

manga (MAHN-gah) Japanese comics.

matsuri (mat-SUH-ree) Festival.

Meiji (MAY-jee) Name given to the reign of the Meiji emperor who ruled from 1867 to 1912 and who helped transform Japan from an isolated agricultural nation to a fledgling world power.

miso paste (MEE-so PAYST) A paste made from soybeans. It goes well with meat, fish, and vegetables and is used widely as a flavoring in fried and broiled dishes and in salad dressing.

nationalist (NASH-nul-ist) Someone who supports the interests and culture of a particular nation.

okonomiyaki sauce (oh-KO-no-me-yak-ee SAHS) A tasty, thick, sweet soy sauce used for okonomiyaki, yakisoba noodles, and fried vegetable dishes.

sake (SAH-kee) Japanese rice wine.

samisen (SAH-mee-sen) Japanese instrument with three strings, which is shaped like a banjo.

samurai (SA-moo-rye) Japanese warrior.

soba (SOO-bah) Buckwheat noodles used in Japanese cooking.

tanka (TAN-ka) Japanese five-line poem of 5, 7, 5, 7, and 7 syllables per line.

Taoism (DOW-ism) A Chinese philosophy that emphasizes living simply and in harmony with nature.

Tokugawa (TOH-kew-gah-wa) Japanese family that controlled Japan from 1603 to 1867. The Tokugawas closed off Japan from the rest of the world for more than two centuries.

tonkatsu sauce (tahn-KAT-soo SAHS) A sauce made of apple, tomato, onion, water, vinegar, sugar, salt, and spices used for chicken and pork dishes.

vigilante (vij-il-AHN-tay) A person who takes the law into his own hands instead of relying on government or local law authorities.

FOR MORE INFORMATION

Kyoto National Museum
527 Chayamachi, Higashiyama-ku
Kyoto, Japan 605-0931
Web site: http://www.kyohaku.go.jp/
   indexe.htm

Tokyo National Museum
13-9 Ueno Park
Taitoku, Tokyo 110-8712
Web site: http://www.tnm.jp/scripts/
   Index.en.idc

Web Sites

Due to the changing nature of Internet links, the Rosen Publishing Group, Inc., has developed an online list of Web sites related to the subject of this book. This site is updated regularly. Please use this link to access the list:

http://www.rosenlinks.com/pswc/japa

FOR FURTHER READING

Behnke, Alison. *Japan in Pictures*. Minneapolis, MN: Lerner Publications Company, 2003.

Haviland, Virginia. Illustrated by Carol Inouye. *Favorite Fairy Tales Told in Japan*. New York: Beech Tree Books, 1996.

Heinrichs, Ann. *Japan*. New York: Children's Press, 1997.

Kimmel, Eric. Illustrated by Michael Graus. *Sword of the Samurai: Adventure Stories from Japan*. New York: Harper Trophy, 2000.

Schomp, Virginia. *Japan in the Days of the Samurai*. New York: Benchmark Books, 1998.

Scoones, Simon. *A Family From Japan*. Austin: Raintree Steck Vaughan, 1998.

Shelley, Rex. *Japan*. New York: Benchmark Books, 1994.

Zurlo, Tony. *Japan: Superpower of the Pacific*. New York: Dillon Press, 1991.

BIBLIOGRAPHY

Cortazzi, Sir Hugh. *Modern Japan: A Concise Survey.* New York: St. Martin's Press, 1999.

Dolan, Edward F., Jr., and Shan Finney. *The New Japan.* New York: Franklin Watts, 1983.

Henshall, Kenneth G. *A History of Japan: From Stone Age to Superpower.* New York: St. Martin's Press, 1999.

Mason, R. H. P. *History of Japan.* New York: Charles E. Tuttle Co., 1988.

Morton, W. Scott. *Japan: Its History and Culture.* New York: McGraw-Hill, 1984.

Perez, Louis G. *The History of Japan.* Westport, CT: Greenwood Publishing Group, 1998.

Schirokauer, Conrad. *A Brief History of Chinese and Japanese Civilizations.* New York: International Thomson Publishing, 1988.

Sugimoto, Yoshio. *An Introduction to Japanese Society.* New York: Cambridge University Press, 1977.

Varley, Paul. *Japanese Culture.* Honolulu: University of Hawaii Press, 2000.

PRIMARY SOURCE IMAGE LIST

Page 9: A woodcut print by Hokusai Katsusika illustrating a poem by Gontchunagon Masafusa.

Page 10 (bottom): *Legend of Zelda* graphic from a Nintendo game. Dated August 25, 2000.

Page 11: Photograph of restaurant in Ryogiku, Tokyo, that used to be part of a sumo wrestling ring. Dated August 1, 1996.

Page 12: Aerial view of field of rice paddies in Shiga, Japan. Photographed by Mitsuhiko Imamori.

Page 14: October 4, 1923, photograph showing earthquake devastation of the Ginza district in Tokyo.

Page 18: May 2000 photo by David Campbell from top of sacred Mount Misen on the island of Miyajima.

Page 22: May 2000 photo by David Campbell of maiko walking in Kiomizu district of Kyoto.

Page 23: Circa 1945 photo of six kamikaze pilots.

Page 24: Photo of Jomon period pottery, dating from 1000 to 200 BC. From the Kimbell Art Museum in Fort Worth, Texas.

Page 25 (top): Circa 1950 photo of Ainu woman in traditional clothing.

Page 26 (bottom): Heian period Fan printed with excerpts from the Lotus Sutra. Dated circa 1150–1185.

Page 27: Circa 1860 photo albumen print of samurai with sword by Felice Beato. From the Stapleton Collection.

Page 28 (top): Circa seventeenth-century painted screen depicting the arrival of the Portuguese called *The Portugeuses.* From Musée des Arts Asiatiques, Paris.

Page 28 (bottom): Lithograph by Sarony Lithography Company of Matthew Perry, circa 1853 to 1855. Housed at the National Portrait Gallery, Smithsonian Institution, Washington, D.C.

Page 29 (bottom): Late nineteenth-century color woodblock print of Emperor Mutsuhito. From Archives Charmet.

Page 32: Photograph of destruction caused by 1945 Hiroshima bomb. By Wayne Miller.

Page 33 (top): Photograph of warning letter to people of Japan, dated August 7, 1945.

Page 34: Circa 1928 photograph of Emperor Hirohito in England.

Page 35: A young couple in Meiji-jinju Park in Tokyo. Photo dated May 2000, by Annie Sommers.

Page 38 (top): Mid-seventeenth-century Edo period scroll featuring calligraphy. Housed in the British Museum, London.

Page 40 (bottom): Twelfth-century drawing of great calligrapher Tofu Ono.

Page 42: Circa 1885 hanging scroll *Izanami and Izanagi Creating the Islands* (of Japan). By Kobayashi Eitaku.

Page 44: Photograph of the wedded rocks at Futamigaura in Ise Bay.

Page 46: Scene from the life of Okinawa Mara (Little Demon) from a twelfth-century woodblock print by Hokkei Toyota.

Page 49: Circa 1858 woodcut of Tamamo-no-Mae (Jewel Maiden) by Utagawa Kunisada.

Page 50: Photograph of elderly woman and dog in Takayama. Dated May 2000, by Annie Sommers.

Page 51: Detail of painted scroll, circa 1185 to 1333, depicting hungry ghosts.

Page 53: Photo of Buddhist festival in 2000 at the Gengoji Temple in Nara.

Page 61: Photo by Abbas of Inari Taisha shrine in Kyoto, 2000.

Page 63: Photo dated September 1, 1993, by Robb Kendrick of the largest shimenawa (rice straw rope) in the oldest Japanese Shinto shrine in Izumo.

Page 66: Sixteenth-century folding screen of St. Francis Xavier and his entourage arriving in Japan. Housed at the Musée Guimet, Paris.

Page 70 (top): Early twelfth-century poetry (calligraphy) from the Osaragi Jiro Collection.

Page 70 (bottom): Ink landscape drawing by Sesshu (1420–1506). From a private collection in Paris.

Page 71 (top): Eleventh-century silk painting from the Temple of Yakushi, in Nara, depicting hanging scroll of Jioin Daishi, founder of Hosso sect.

Page 72: Ando Hiroshige woodcut dated circa 1833 to 1834 from series called 53 Stages of the Tokaido. Collection of the Newark Museum.

Page 73 (top): Photograph of Haniwa horse sculpture found near Boshu province. From Dolmen period. Housed in National Museum of Scotland.

Page 73 (bottom): Photograph of Jizo on fiftieth anniversary of atomic bomb blast in Hiroshima. Dated 1995, Philip Jones Griffiths.

Page 74: Gold and red nineteenth-century boxes. From the Oriental Art Museum in Genoa, Italy.

Page 77: Micheal S. Yamahita photo of the exterior of Osaka Castle, dated June 1988.

Page 80: 1984 photo of Kabuki actor Ebizo in Tokyo. Image by Burt Glinn.

Page 82 (top): Surimono circa 1795 to 1804. Housed at the British Museum, London.

Page 82 (bottom): Circa 1615 to 1868 calligraphy painting (Waka-shikishi) by Koetsu and Sotatsu.

Page 84: Portrait of author Yukio Mishima at home in Tokyo, September 10, 1966. Image by Masaki Nobuyuki.

Page 85: Manga poster of *Inu-Yasha: A Feudal Fairy Tale*. Story and art by Rumiko Takahashi.

Page 87: Circa 1573 to 1615 Momoyama period Noh mask.

Page 89: Circa 1890 painting of Kabuki actor Danjuro Ickikawa performing as Benkei in *Kanjincho* (The Subscription List).

Page 96: August 1, 1996, photo of sumo match at Kokugikan stadium in Tokyo.

Page 97: Scene from animated film *Spirited Away*, by Hayao Miyazaki. Dated November 2, 2002.

Page 100 (bottom): Circa 1895 drawing of Buddhist monks and women in Japanese costume.

Page 102 (top): Movie scene from 1955 film *Godzilla*.

Page 102 (bottom): Movie still of Akira Kurosawa's *Seven Samurai*, featuring Toshiro Mifune.

Page 105: May 2000 photograph of children at Peace Memorial Park in Hiroshima. Image by David Campbell.

Page 113: May 2000 photo of commemorative plaque at Peace Memorial Park in Hiroshima. Image by David Campbell.

INDEX

About the Author
Meg Greene is an author living in Virginia.

Designer: Geri Fletcher; **Cover Designer:** Tahara Anderson;
Editor: Annie Sommers; **Photo Researcher:** Fernanda Rocha